JULY, 1964

This endpaper map adapted from original four-color version prepared for
the City of Compton by Wilsey & Ham
of Los Angeles.

Also by Richard M. Elman

THE POORHOUSE STATE: *The American Way of Life on Public Assistance*

ILL-AT-EASE IN COMPTON

ILL-AT-EASE IN COMPTON

RICHARD M. ELMAN

PANTHEON BOOKS

A Division of Random House

New York

"In the making of the American image
abroad, people . . . with their private
preoccupations, are given no part. But
they are important because there are so
many of them; and because they are
necessarily insulated people."

Susan Cooper, *Behind the Golden
Curtain*, Charles Scribner's Sons, 1966,
p. 106.

AUTHOR'S NOTE

As the reader will learn, I went to Compton with the thought in mind that this was *the* future. It is what lies in store for all the new suburbs of all the big cities of America. Southern California lends itself to this. It is, after all, the greatest megalopolis in the most populous state of the nation. What happens there happens elsewhere sooner or later. Just as the emergence of the Negro in the suburbs happened first in California, it is bound to happen elsewhere—when the Negro masses begin to find some measure of economic stability—and, in general, one doesn't have to be a Nostradamus to observe that, more and more, California's experience filters itself back across the country. Carey McWilliams (who knows the state as well as anybody) calls it a great "forcing ground," but it is so even more than that metaphor seems to suggest. It is the future which the

Californian Lincoln Steffens left behind to go to Russia, and observe "I have seen the future and it works."

Who knows? In some not-too-distant future, it may even be what Russians have to look forward to.

ACKNOWLEDGMENTS

My travel and research expenses for this book were
generously covered under a grant from the Stern Family
Fund. My thanks go to David Hunter, who acted promptly
and without undue formality on my request for the grant.

To the many people of Compton who assisted and
advised me, I am deeply thankful, and also to Mrs. Carolyn
Bloomberg of the A.C.L.U. of Los Angeles, for her warm
and efficient hospitality and assistance.

Ill-At-Ease in Compton uses false identities for real
people, and some place names have been changed as well.
It is written for my daughter Margaret.

CONTENTS

COMPTON

A BRIEF HISTORY OF EVENTS AND POPULATION GROWTH*

Compton, thirteenth-largest incorporated city in Los Angeles County, has an estimated population at present of 75,000. Here are some milestones in its history:

May, 1883:   Founding of Women's Christian Temperance Union, and construction of building at northeast corner of Culver Street and Lemon Street (Compton Boulevard).

May 11, 1888:   Election and formal incorporation of Compton as a city of the sixth class.

July 28, 1888:   First issue of The Compton Independent.

January 11, 1904:   Beginning of regular instruction in new building at Compton Union High School.

November 14, 1904:   Organization of Our Lady of Victory parish of the Roman Catholic Church.

May 10, 1924:   Opening of Compton Airport, at Olive Street (Alondra Boulevard) and Wilmington Avenue.

June 6, 1924:   First issue of The Compton News.

December 9, 1924: Approval, at a general freeholders election, of a city manager form of government.

April 9, 1925:   Official chartering of the Kiwanis Club of Compton.

* This listing is drawn, in part, from "The Story of a City, Compton, California, 1888–1963," a pamphlet published by the Diamond Jubilee Committee of the City of Compton and the Compton Chamber of Commerce in 1963.

March 10, 1933: Earthquake.

April 16, 1947: Dedication of the "Eagle Tree" by Compton Parlor # 258, Native Daughters of The Golden West, at a corner of Poppy and Short Streets.

1963: Construction of Compton Shopping Center.

August 11, 1965: Riots break out in neighboring Watts and Willowbrook, leaving 35 dead, 1,032 injured, 600 buildings damaged by burning and looting, more than $40 million in property irretrievably damaged, and a state of emergency is declared in Compton during which over 100 persons are eventually incarcerated.

Selected Index of Population Growth:

  1910: 922

  1932: 14,900

  1945: 26,294

  1963: 75,000

1

"IT'S MOSTLY COLORED"

All of Los Angeles County seemed to be under a poison gas attack of brownish low-lying clouds beyond which I could barely make out a cool greenish-bluish mandala composed of thousands of odd-shaped bits of turquoise. A wind rocked the plane, brushing some of the clouds to one side so that, under glinting sun, the turquoise pattern stood out even more boldly. It was as if a great egalitarian gesture of some giant hand had passed across the city, tossing out those little pieces of semiprecious stone in one formless sweep over flatlands and canyons, on the sheared-off humps of the man-made mesas and adjacent to the freeways, until they gave the illusion of being almost everywhere.

Almost but not quite! Moments after the "No Smoking" sign blinked on in the front of our cabin, I glanced down

nervously and first noticed them, among the scattered habi-
tations of one of the sunny valleys—and then I promptly
lost them again, as we crossed a seemingly uninhabited
range of hills thick with madrone. Discolored drafts of air
passed my cabin window, as we crossed to the other side of
the mountain range where, again, those thousands of gem-
like specks jammed against one another, making my vision
stammer. Some were symmetrical, others amoebic or trape-
zoidal, or set among what seemed to be circlets of colored
tiles. The total density of the pattern was by now quite
astonishing. I had crossed over a great nowhere into something quite unique. Just as I turned to ask my neighbor
on the left if he knew what all this was, the plane banked
sharply back on its course. The man smiled: "I live down
there. I bet I can find my pool."

"It's shaped like a bow-tie," he said, brushing across me
as he leaned over my seat (so that I got the full aroma of
his spiced lime after-shave lotion) and then lapsed back
again, disappointed: "It's a shame. I have a really nice
place. We must have gone too far south."

Remembering then that Los Angeles County had more
pools and more farms than any other urban center in the
world, I glanced down across the wings of the plane once
again. We were crossing back over the sprawl the way we
had come and the pools reflected the late May sun, but
nobody seemed to be splashing about anywhere. So here
were all those thousands of vacant pools at midday in the
fierce burning sun, in the midst of traffic; and now that I
knew what they were, it all seemed rather queer, as if the

4

entire city had fled before that invasion of strange metallic bugs proceeding along the elevated freeways. The further downtown we penetrated the more this uncanny sense of empty dusty idleness was emphasized. The traffic thickened until it seemed like a thin extruded line without motion, and our plane drifted along, worrying the brightly lit ground with a shadow which always seemed to be advancing on it at a rapid pace. Why wasn't anybody taking a dip anywhere? Why did we always seem to be circling in and out of that same poisonous cloud bank, above that same dusty pile of glitter? When I suddenly announced to my neighbors that I was going to Compton and wondered aloud which direction that would be, a patch of blue sea popped into view, and my neighbor at the left glanced at me coldly, as if, by uttering such a place name, I had abruptly declassed myself before his eyes. Then the woman on my right, who I sensed had been eavesdropping, remarked: "It's mostly colored there."

Glancing about the plane, the man added: "I wouldn't say that. I used to drive to Compton for the relay races. At one time they were just about the best in the country. Now they hold them at the Coliseum. But I don't think that has anything to do with the colored."

"Or with Watts?"

"No ma'am, I don't think so."

"It's a lot safer in the Coliseum."

"I wouldn't say that either," the man said. "A lot of top Negroes happen to live in Compton. You would be surprised at the number of nice homes and pools."

5

"That's what my husband says," the woman smiled. "Well, if that's the case, what are they complaining about?"

"I don't know that they are," the man said, trying to be sweetly reasonable. "Has there been any trouble in Compton?"

"*I meant Watts*," the woman declared, turning to her window again. But she turned back quickly: "Honestly, it's so exasperating, those people. It's nearly a year later and this is all I can ever talk about."

"It isn't that bad," the man said. "I wouldn't want to give that impression."

"Maybe not for you. It is for me. I guess you just don't remember what it was like."

"I remember."

"Sure, I'll bet you do."

"I just don't think," the man swallowed his Adam's apple, "that you're being very fair."

"Why should I?"

There was a long pause bruised with silence during which even the plane seemed preternaturally still. Then the back-lash tongue-lashing started up once again across my lap while I pretended to be searching for Disneyland in the sprawl. And because the rooftops of tracts, industrial parks, and little cities, which we were then passing over, all seemed so much alike, pool-spotting was as good a way as any that I had of dispelling that kind of aimless race talk, of quieting my own uncertainties about where I was heading, of recalling Compton—a place I had only visited once

about four years ago—and tallying my recollection against
those slanderous images of the place. Finally, it became a
way of finding my bearings above that huge directionless
mass, of sorting out the solidly middle-class districts of LA
from the shabby enclaves toward which I knew I would be
heading.

I checked myself against my map memories, asked myself
was this place Gardena and that place South Gate. But we
were now crossing over a long blighted corridor of little
boxlike bungalows and smoking factories, and the number of
turquoise specks suffered an immediate decline. Now I
could pick out many black spots, the scabs of fires, whole
blocks of blackened rubble, the remains, no doubt, of those
gutted buildings I had read about the previous August.
Then, we flew over the racetrack at Inglewood—and then
another concentration of pools. It was rather exhilarating;
each little habitation seemed to be giving off its own cool
little glow. Staring down myopically at those streets dotted
with turquoise, I felt our plane make a sudden drop low
for a landing. "You take care of yourself," the man said;
my woman neighbor pushed her way past us as we stood in
the aisle minutes later, waiting for the carpeted exit tunnel
to be jammed into place. Then the door swung open and I
looked down the long corrugated tube toward the fluores-
cent corridors of the terminal. A pretty Negro stewardess
was smiling at me: "Have a pleasant trip?"

An hour later I was to learn another foolproof way of
locating the shabby neighborhoods of LA when, after
registering at a downtown hotel for that night only, I went

out into the flashing day to look for a car to rent. The air
had a faint burnt taste, as if someone were lighting a pile
of twigs nearby, and a fine hot needle of sun kept jabbing
at the space between my eyes. At a shack advertising Volks-
wagens a small clerk signed me up for the special-discount
monthly contract, which was still more than I had wanted
to spend, and then frowned when I asked directions to
Compton. From the way he sneered when I said the name,
it was as if I had inquired about the nearest camel caravan
route to Stockton when, in fact, I knew that I was at that
very moment standing no more than ten miles away from
Compton City Hall. "I used to live in Torrance," the clerk
said at last, "and I was glad to get away from there."

I asked just what had been so wrong with Torrance.

"Wrong?" he asked. "Who said anything about wrong?
I just said I was glad to get out of there.

"Anyway," he added, "if you're headed that way, just be
sure to drive away from the mountains. That way you can't
ever get lost." He cracked open a road map, glanced at it,
folded it back again in a messy packet, and pushed it across
the counter.

"Why anybody would want to go to Compton is a mystery to me," he said. When I still refused to enlighten him,
he handed me the road map and smiled: "You can get lost
very easily in this town if you don't know how to drive
yourself around."

"Once I get there," I said, "I intend to stay there."

Now the clerk seemed thoroughly disgusted with me: "I
don't think you'll like it down there. It's all flat . . . full of

smog. I live out in Santa Monica in the hills. That's the only really livable part of town. No smog." He surrendered the car keys and pointed out my tomato-red Volkswagen: "My mother used to work near Compton during the war. You know who was born there?"

"You tell me," I said.

He was leering: "Tokyo Rose. It caused a great big stink when she turned traitor. I remember it like it was only yesterday. You remember Tokyo Rose, don't you? Well, her father was a Nisei farmer. There were lots of Japs down there at one time. So she turned out to be pro-Jap. It was just one of those things. I can't say I blame her. But Compton really was chicken shit in those days. After the war, they had this big Americanism crusade for the kids. My mother said I had to go. It was a big thing. A guy named Kid Mexico Faulkner used to take full-page ads in the shopping papers. He was going to do something about all the juvenile delinquency . . . teach kids respect. Finally, they caught him running a keeno game. I can't imagine what Compton must be like today. I guess it's all colored."

"Every bit of it?" I asked.

"An awful lot, I bet."

Having seen my driver's license, he knew I was from New York. As I was about to leave, he made one final effort to discourage me: "Don't let any of those rednecks catch you with a colored girl."

"I thought you said it was all colored."

"What isn't colored," the clerk said, "is redneck." He paused so that his little aphorism might sink in. Then:

"Most people from the East don't like that kind of place."

"It's business," I explained.

"I thought it was," the fellow smirked. "Although, you'd be surprised. We get an awful lot of tourists going down that way. They go to see Watts. It's right next door to Watts . . . Watts and Compton, I mean."

I said I already knew that.

"Anyway," he said, "remember what I said about the hills and that way you'll never get lost."

That advice proved to be as useful as his previous efforts at deterrence. Twenty minutes later, after making all the correct turns on all the right streets, I was snarled in a great horse-hitch knot of traffic on a freeway that wound through hill country, and all around me were the shacks of poor Mexicans. Obviously, something had gone terribly wrong somewhere, but, at that moment, my anger was necessarily unfocused. The heat kept needling me. My six foot five inches were folded inside the Volkswagen so that my knees were almost level with my shoulders. And when the traffic came unstuck, there seemed to be no way I could turn back. One just had to keep on rolling. But the further I went, the more those hills proliferated and the bleaker was the surrounding prospect. Not even a clump of madrone could take root along that empty dusty stretch of little shacks under palmettos and dry hills shorn off at the top and scarred with unpaved trails. Behind some hurricane fencing, an oil pump genuflected slowly. Nearby, a family was selling nightcrawlers. I seemed to have entered a desperate *favela* in a section of Los Angeles I had never seen before, and there was no way to go except to climb forward. I even had trouble getting over to a lane from which I might exit. Every time I tried to do so a giant trailer truck loomed up against the rear-view mirror to bleat its horn at me like an enraged stag.

Presently this freeway seemed to branch out into a ganglion of lesser turnpikes. Signs were sprouting everywhere. Not one pointed to Compton. But somewhere nearby was Dodger Stadium, according to a little blue and white disc bending toward the soft shoulder. For a moment I wondered if Koufax might be pitching. If so, it would be worth taking the afternoon off rather than having to put up with any more traffic. I switched on the radio:

A woman was shouting over a telephone: "Watts! Watts! Watts! Can't you ever feel sorry for anybody else? If they want to give those people a hospital, that's all right with me. They'll only burn it down anyway . . . and why do I have to pay for that?"

I turned to another station: "It's our son," a tired voice was saying, "we're pretty sure he's a user only we don't know what he uses."

On a third station the announcer interrupted a whiny voice and said: "You're pretty insignificant anyway," hanging up his phone just as a commercial began: "Ladies, if you've got maggots in your garbage cans, here's a sure-fire way to get rid of them."

Finally, I settled for Frank Sinatra as the long file of cars, of which I was now an inseparable element, continued to race through a flatter area of small factories and ugly

11

pistachio bungalows. "From dawn to dusk, nothing but Frankyboy," said a voice of the exact timbre of a nail file rubbing against putty. Then I noticed how one road seemed to be curving back again toward the direction from which I'd come, and how there were still others forking off of it like pieces of telephone cable. Stepping down hard on the gas pedal so that I could make the turn, I found the roads branching out toward another set of hills and canyons, but, within minutes, I was back at the Civic Center once more.

I rode off the freeway and parked the car beneath the overhead so that I could get out to stretch my legs. The traffic was like surf above my head and my sport clothes were now soaked through, the fabric like fire where it was still dry and like a damp diaper elsewhere. Standing, then, under the shadows of whatever they called that freeway, it occurred to me that after all these years I might never even get to Compton again. Then I wondered why I even thought I had to go there. Why me? Why Compton?

CHAPTER II

ILL-AT-EASE IN COMPTON

I first became interested in Compton about four years ago when I was working as a free-lance script writer for educational television. We were preparing a series on American voting behavior to serve as a kind of primer on politics for the Goldwater-Johnson election campaign; our Washington research consultants, working with raw census data and polling returns, had recommended that we select two California towns—one predominantly Democratic and the other Republican—and attempt to show what was sociologically distinctive about the voting behavior of these two communities. How Compton was selected to be the Democratic community must, I'm afraid, remain obscure. All I know is that I was ordered to catch the first plane out to Compton, weeks in advance of our camera crews, so as to select sites, interview prominent personalities, gather data, and prepare a treatment and, subsequently, a shooting script on the theme of why Compton tended to vote overwhelmingly Democratic. The local Chamber of Commerce representative, who later turned out to be a pleasant red-faced former army noncom from Alabama, told me over long-distance telephone, when I announced our plans: "Sure we'll co-operate, but I think you're going to be in for a pretty big surprise." And when I arrived a few days later at his office, he added: "Didn't I tell you that you were in for a surprise?"

Unfortunately, my superiors in New York were very surprised indeed (in fact, they were appalled) when I reported back that evening that Compton's Democratic strength* in recent years was chiefly attributable to the fact that Negroes populated it to the extent of nearly 50 per cent. I also indicated that our program would surely have to consider this factor in seeking to draw any meaningful profile of the community. "Impossible," my producer snapped back. "We just can't do that."

When I asked him to explain why, he said: "Because it just wouldn't be a typical American town. I asked for Main Street USA and you've given us Harlem."

I said: "You're paying those damned fools all that money and they don't even know if there are Negroes there or not," and then became offended with myself, as well as with him. After having spent a week visiting people in their homes and offices, could I honestly tell myself—or anybody

* Gerrymandering has, nevertheless, resulted in Compton's helping to elect a Republican congressman throughout most of the past decade.

14

else, for that matter—that Compton was just like Harlem? Why should Compton have seemed any less typical to me than, say, the Brooklyn I had known as a small boy? Besides, whoever said that Main Street ever really existed to begin with?

But when I protested that the homes were neat and the schools well attended, even though there was a certain amount of blight and waste and perhaps too many Negro men standing on street corners, my boss, in New York, became increasingly distraught: "I don't care what you say. If it's 50 per cent black, it just is not a typical American town."

I asked, "Have you got any other places in mind?"

"I have my orders," he said. "It will have to be Compton. We're just too late to make substitutions. So why don't you just sit tight and we'll send somebody out who knows how to talk to these people and their leaders. And, in the meantime, try to think of ways we can shoot around some of those Negroes."

Shoot around the Negroes! Negro experts! I got myself prepared to greet a man who would be a combination of Daniel P. Moynihan and Adolf Eichmann. But it turned out to be not quite that bad. Eventually, it was just another piece of skulduggery in that long, squalid chronicle known as broadcasting history. Two days later the network vice-president, a former State Department foreign-aid functionary, arrived, and he ordered me to chauffeur him once around through the streets of Compton. Afterwards, we repaired to an air-conditioned steak restaurant, and this

15

expert on African poverty declared what are probably memorable words: "These are happy Negroes."

"Yes," he murmured, considering the weight of his remarks, "these are no doubt happy Negroes, so I just don't see what people are panicking about." But, in the end, we only did a few days' lickety-split shooting in Compton, trying our best to frame as many white folks into every shot as possible, and then we went on as soon as we could to our solidly Republican town, where we made every effort possible to shoot around that town's chief subculture, the John Birch Society.

Afterwards, the vice-president questioned me closely as he prepared to board a jet back to New York: "Didn't I tell you they were happy Negroes? I can't honestly understand what people were so panicked about! Anybody could see they were happy. Couldn't you?" But one month later, most of the euphoria which he had extracted from Compton's Negro population was excised on the cutting room floor, and the educationalists presented a portrait of the typical American voter that was as bland as it was boring and as boring as it was white.

That slightly disingenuous phrase, happy Negroes, didn't enter my consciousness again until the summer of 1965, when I was en route to Europe with my family. Suddenly one morning the ship's newspaper and closed-circuit television (on which important events in the world outside were broadcast in stolid Anglo-Dutch) were full of battle reports and casualty lists from a place called Watts. The

alarm aboard ship was soon contagious: In first-class, pas-
sengers started muttering to one another about *The Fire
Next Time* as they turned their faces up to the warm At-
lantic sun. In tourist class, meanwhile, I heard many young
students congratulating themselves for having said it would
happen all along; and, of course, the foreigners were snick-
ering quite a bit about American racism. As the news report
continued like muffled drums, interrupting all efforts at con-
viviality, the riots were continually described as if they
were happening in the Watts area (with Watts itself made to
seem like some remote community off by itself), which only
increased my anxieties about my friends in Compton. Was
it also being engulfed in flames? Or was it a bastion of
solidly middle-class support for the police? Were there
National Guardsmen now stationed in front of the Los
Angeles Memorial Mausoleum with bayonets pointed up
toward those fierce gold minarets? What was my friend
from Alabama doing and thinking? And what about all
those putatively "happy Negroes"?

I never learned much more until weeks after we'd docked,
when I came upon a flame-red copy of *Paris Match* in the
toilet of a *relais* near Bordeaux; and, by then, I had to try
to push it to the back of my mind and concentrate on my
work. A year spent on another book then intervened, and
when I was finished, I told my editor about my obsession
with the town of Compton. "I'd like to go back and know
what happened," I said.

There followed an exchange of letters, and in another

17

fortnight I was assured an advance and a small grant to cover my travel expenses, and I was on the way.

．　　．　　．

But why Compton?

Most American cities have something about which they can boast. Although many of these reputations were acquired years ago, they manage to linger on: Either such places manufacture carpets or shirt collars, market garlic or apples, or perhaps they house a distinguished college, a major store, or an insurance firm. As far as I know, Compton can boast that it has none of these things. Until recently, it was just a sovereign city of over 75,000 people which, in the general LA boom, had tripled its population in the last two decades, lying right on the other side of Watts, in an area that was once all bean fields. Geographically, Compton lies in the southern-central section of what the *Los Angeles Times* calls "Southland," about halfway between downtown LA and the port of Long Beach-San Pedro, and maybe that's why they call it "Hub City." In Compton's case, just exactly what being at the hub signifies has been left unspecified.

Not that its size is unimpressive. In some of our western states an agglomeration of 75,000 persons living, for the most part, in private homes, might constitute a town of some note, but in rapidly growing California it is just what it seems to be and nothing more: another bunch of tracts and stores and schools and small factories, and a junior college, formed around the bare bones of a municipal government which collects taxes, polices streets, passes on permits and beautification ordinances, and lends its support to a number of civic-minded groups such as the Elks, the Lions, the Rotarians, and the Chamber of Commerce. More often than not, the people living there may work in some other similar town nearby, or even quite far away. Compton? It's just a bedroom. Probably it even lacks the charm of, say, Yonkers.

And, as with pretty nearly all the other seventy-five incorporated cities of more or less the same size in a Los Angeles metropolitan area of over seven million people, the inhabitants of Compton are governed in some of their affairs by other bare bones assemblages such as county supervisors, state legislatures, municipal water boards, independently financed school boards, and they exist—for the most part—in a relatively benign anarchy of private homes, private cars, and private ambitions. Public higher education is available for nearly everybody, and the worst thing that one can say of some Compton families these days is that they house a school drop-out. But that is probably just as true, if not truer, of the families of La Canada or Huntington Park, Lakewood, or South Gate. The pastel boxes housing the tract dwellers of Compton are not startlingly different from those of Lynwood, Bell, or Paramount. The used-car lots on Long Beach Boulevard could be duplicated in the San Fernando Valley. In Compton's better districts, there are the same two-story, mission-style homes with ornamental bitter orange trees on their lawns as there are in the residential sections of Santa Monica or the Beverly Fairfax section of LA or even some of the less remote Hollywood hills.

Architecturally, Los Angeles is a rather avant-garde city, the ultimate recapitulation of the theme of greed which in its rather garish variations and numerous suburban nuances recapitulates itself even more garishly and constantly until the old distinctions of class and status, of town and city, are a blur. "The more I lived in LA, the less I knew about America," the hero of Clancy Sigal's *Going Away* reflects, "even when I knew that LA was some sort of crazy portent and advance guard for the whole thing we call the United States of America." And indeed it is! Heaven help us all if Paris doesn't look that way some day. It almost does now around Passy and Neuilly. But, if you've never been to either place, visit your newest and most futuristic shopping center and then multiply it by the thousands and you'll have a fairly suitable image of what to expect, or, better yet, imagine that somebody has taken your daughter seriously as a city planner just because she happened to make all her blocks stand up straight.

But, though LA is a hodge-podge of such proportions that it often seems strangulated by its own disorders, one comes to recognize an order to the whole mess. Race, caste, and ethnic groups still impose their invisible orders on the human spirit. Old Jews live in Venice, the young in Brentwood, and hardly any of them live in Compton. In the Dominguez hills to the north of Compton are the same

oil wells that one finds pumping along the beaches of
squalid Venice because the serpents of black wealth beneath the soil seem to coil every way, across every boundary.
And if all the incorporated cities are, by state law, uni-
formly nonpartisan, it no longer seems to matter that some
are inhabited chiefly by Democrats (i.e., Compton),
whereas others are Republican enclaves (i.e., Pasadena); in
California, Democrats—many of whom are newcomers
from the South and Southwest—can often be more conservative than some Republicans, as the recent election of
Ronald Reagan proved once again. Los Angeles is random-
ness, mindlessness, disorder to the point of madness, but
within such anarchy everything conspires to a seeming
uniformity, an enforced order. What, if anything, are the
distinctions one can make?

A census along Rosecrantz Boulevard might indicate that
Compton has more Wienerschnitzel stands than Mac-
Donald Burgers (whereas the reverse might be true along
Alondra near Torrance), but this is hardly a measurement
of significance. Nor can one make too much of the fact
that the local columbarium and mausoleum is phony
Moorish with minarets and a gold-leaf onion dome on the
roof rather than, say, mock-Colonial, as it is in one of the
Pasadena Hills. What sets Compton apart from Paramount, Lakewood, Lynwood, Bell, or South Gate is its increasing blackness. This is a community which is now more
than 50 per cent Negro. Or, as the local papers put it,
"minority group." But if you are part of the 50 per cent
who are black, it's increasingly difficult to think of yourself

21

as part of a minority group. Unless, of course, you've been made to think so.

"There are no two ways about it," the astute Negro attorney, editor, and now municipal court judge, Loren Miller, wrote in his newspaper, *The California Eagle*, as far back as 1961: "If Los Angeles County insists on putting up with all-white cities it is going to have to face the spectacle of all-Negro cities." He was talking about a Compton which then had a Negro population of 40.2 per cent. Miller found the prospect of increased migration by Negroes to Compton disquieting: "I doubt that there are any other cities of Compton's size (North or South) that can boast—if that's the word—a comparable percentage. And the end isn't in sight. Unless the trend is stopped, and there's nothing in sight to stop it, Compton is going to become an all-Negro city."

Just what is so disquieting about the prospects of an "all-Negro" suburb remains to be explored. I grew up in a virtually all-Jewish neighborhood of "minority-group" Brooklyn and found it, if anything, rather reassuring. But what is equally odd is that Loren Miller then thought the solution to the "plight" of Compton lay in open-housing legislation, whereas it was Compton's reluctant acceptance of "minority group" open-housing demands, and the failure of other neighboring cities to do even that much, which was partly responsible for the present in-migration.*

* Between 1950 and 1960, Compton's white population declined by 18.5 per cent, while nonwhites were increasing by 165 per cent, according to the Welfare Planning Council of Los Angeles publication entitled "Compton: A Community in Transition."

If you were to look at a map of south-central Los Angeles, it would be plain why this was so; Compton's eight square miles are contiguous to that huge blighted area which now goes by the name of Watts, but Compton is not a slum—by any means. While 42 per cent of the Watts male population is so unemployed, according to a recent State of California Labor Department survey, that it has dropped out of the labor force entirely, average family incomes in Compton are only about $500 less than in Los Angeles County in general; and LA is considerably above the nationwide average. Thus, the bulk of Compton's Negro population seems safely lower-middle class, at least in income; they are postmen, blue-collar workers, teachers, etc., and one would think that if ever the enforced togetherness of race could be transformed into a positive thing, Compton would be such a place. And that is, apparently, what many Negroes were thinking when they came to Compton.

This reasonable stability of income is also the real source of lower-middle-class black power. If a Negro can afford to get out of Watts (and he hasn't quite got the income or the class to live in an integrated area such as the Baldwin Hills), he will usually turn southward toward Compton and environs to buy his home because, since the 1950's, it has been made rather easy for him to do so. But this is no longer the case when he tries to move further east into such relatively lily-white communities as Lynwood, Lakewood, Paramount, and Bell. Further west is Inglewood (which has also rather successfully managed to hold the color line), and somewhat to the south of that is Gardena, an enclave of numerous Orientals. For over a decade, then, the population of the black belt of Los Angeles, seeking liberation from the urban slum, has been pouring through a widening funnel of county strip into Compton. Here, it seems, a man has a chance to find decent housing and educate his children. Here it is possible to enjoy the great lower-middle-class dream of private life without feeling as if one were in a private hell. In the alleyways of Compton's Negro houses, one is likely to see motorboats and campers parked with about the same profusion as in the white neighborhoods; but on Thursday, a black man in an Ivy League suit goes from door to door, dropping copies of *Muhammad Speaks*. Compton, in short, has become a city which sends its Negro high-school graduates to the state colleges, to Berkeley and UCLA, and some even can afford to go as far away as Fisk, the private university in Nashville, Tennessee. Dodger catcher John Roseboro resides in Compton. So do a number of other Negroes who have gained a modicum of success and optimism through their own hard endeavors. As people never tire of telling you: "We're different here than in Watts."

But this assertion is not always as unfettered by the harsh facts of ghetto life as it seems. In generally upper lower-middle-class Compton, 143 persons had to be hauled to jail, including eighty Negro adults who were booked for felonies, as a reverberation of the Watts riots. Compton's racially integrated force of ninety police officers had been schooled in "human relations" seminars, and they acted quickly when Watts started to burn; they hauled in any possible troublemakers and avoided a major disaster—in part because they received so much cooperation from both the black and white residents of Compton—yet the threat of violence was always present in those days; and it is just simply not the case, as some have asserted, that all the troublemakers were from Watts.

Moreover, "Watts" is increasingly used as a cover name for a variety of Negro communities in LA. When a newspaper reporter says Watts, he usually does not mean to refer to the discrete geographical area of the city of Los Angeles which houses the marvelously dreamlike, gaudy towers of Simon Roditi. It is, rather, a euphemism for the entire black-belt complex which begins where the Mexican district dwindles in East Los Angeles and includes the un-incorporated county strips of Enterprise and Willowbrook, and portions of Santa Monica. Though Compton was hardly bruised by the Watts explosion, its next-door neighbor, Willowbrook, was gravely damaged by the fires and the rioting. It was in Willowbrook that Marquette and Ronald Frye were stopped by Los Angeles County Sheriff Lee Minikus in the incident which precipitated the disaster. Willowbrook is also the most immediate extension of Watts itself, not quite a step up in the world, but a step out. Its shacks are sometimes larger than those of Watts. There are a few more well-tended gardens. People in Willowbrook are governed by the county; there is no local autonomy. As a consequence, public services are probably worse here than in Los Angeles proper; the county sheriff may be just a little better than the LA city police. Willowbrook is a community inhabited by many Negroes and Mexicans, nearly all of whom are poor. About all one can say about the prospects of the Willowbrook community is that, thus far, Compton—although anxious to acquire assessable land—has always steadfastly refused to consider its annexation. So, for that matter, has the city of Los Angeles. It is one of those limbos created by Negro poverty which no one, with the possible exception of its residents, wishes to see abolished. Residents of Compton rarely talk about annexing Willowbrook. When a local newspaperman recently made such a suggestion, he prefaced it with a series of apologies to the people of Compton.

When the rioters from Watts and Willowbrook turned toward Compton, they were greeted by the local residents with shotguns, "blood brothers or no blood brothers," but this demonstration of civic responsibility did not make as much of an impression on the white man—or Caucasian, as he is commonly called in California—as one might have thought. By the time Watts rose up, Negro migration to Compton had become such an ugly self-fulfilling prophecy to the white man that, to a large extent, he was no longer around to congratulate his Negro neighbors on their community spirit. And, in the months following Watts, the white out-migration increased: On every block the "for sale" signs appeared. The upper lower-middle-class white man may have been cutting off his nose to spite his face, but he seemed to think it was better to have a face without a nose than no face at all. Panic selling created a glut on the housing market; the number of new building permits that were issued declined sharply. Compton's white city manager began to worry about the financial future of the community, and the generally tight money market in the area (caused in part by the riots, in part by the war in Vietnam, by Negro poverty and white discrimination) made it difficult even for eligible Negroes to purchase homes. But if the white man was fleeing Compton for the outlying areas, the Negro was fleeing Watts for Compton. After the riots, as many as three hundred persons a month continued to come to live in the town; most were Negro renters. In a year the public welfare population had jumped 10 per cent, mostly in the Aid for Dependent Children category.

White liberals and Negro civil rights activists, who had hoped to promote Compton as a kind of model interracial community, have not always known how to confront what has been happening to the Hub City. In Compton, "black power" is more than just a slogan; two out of four city councilmen and the town clerk are Negroes, and the white mayor, an instructor at the local junior college, feels regularly obliged to defer to his Negro electorate by declaring that "once you get to know them, they are just like everybody else" (by which he means that they are lawyers, doctors, etc.). But the fact remains that many of the newcomers are not at all like those whose places they have taken among the white and Negro upper lower-middle-classes. They are much poorer. They live in overcrowded housing and generally have larger families than their predecessors. Some have come directly from the agrarian milieu of the deep South. Others have brought with them the bitterness of the Watts experience. Still others lack jobs of any sort. Their children get into trouble with the law. They have difficulty meeting rent and mortgage payments. They are the chief customers of the bail bondsmen who have been setting up shop all along Compton Boulevard. They, it is said, are the reasons all the Compton stores now sport elaborate systems of thief-detection mirrors. The lengthy charge sheet against the newcomers grows daily. And the result has been the subdivision of Compton into virtually three, or perhaps four, distinct neighborhood entities: a black ghetto in the westernmost portion of town, a white ghetto in its easternmost portion, and, in between, an integrated ghetto.* Moreover, within all three of these ghettos, but within the black ghetto especially, there are discrete but increasingly abject pockets of real poverty, the result, probably, of the blighted patches of housing at low rentals which attract the poor to the area. Compton seems to be getting poorer: aggregate retail sales are going down—not up. The local merchants complain about the new trade and don't bother to renew their leases; and even Compton welfare-state liberals are starting to bellow a good deal about

* By 1960, east Compton was less than 1 per cent nonwhite, west Compton was more than 40 per cent nonwhite, and central Compton was 39 per cent nonwhite, according to the Welfare Planning Council of Los Angeles.

28

"the strain of middle-class wage-earners supporting the disadvantaged."

. . .

Imagine a two-hundred-foot-long shoe box no more than ten feet high, set into an acre and a half of concrete faced with gaudy ceramic trivets which are pasted together with gobs of pastel concrete, and you have a fairly good image of the typical Southern California motel. Usually, it will be surmounted by a mast with semaphore flags. Occasionally, it will be broken in two to form a wedge or a V around its pool. Adjacent to it there may also be a smaller boxlike structure with a placard atop it reading "EAT HERE," and perhaps some of the motel rooms will have tiny, darkly curtained windows abutting the traffic.

And though the designs may vary from location to location, the uninhibited gaudiness and the sense one has of imminent discomfort in boxlike warrens is fairly uniform: a palm tree here, deciduating slowly in the sun; a windbreak of bamboo or eucalyptus along the driveway; the parking lot ample; the renting office, rather tiny and smelling of Airwick and cabbage. The going rate for accommodations at such places is from eight to ten dollars a day and, of course, everything comes wrapped in sanitary tissues: the drinking glasses, the toilet seat, even the pancakes which you are served next door at breakfast.

The motels always seem to appear in clusters. After miles of vacancy at worst, or at best, shops, houses, gas stations and the like, one is besieged by Oases, Haciendas, and Villas ———. In fact, if one of these things looks at all modest or scaled to human beings (say it's only a small concrete building with three or perhaps four units faced with redwood), the chances are that they let apartments, and you can't get sheets or towels.

One drives along from one plasticized cluster of objects to the next, and the price never seems to vary by much. Always one is greeted by a weary old man with a lined face, or by his wife or daughter—the women's hair usually has been dyed blonde—and the air of hard use and wear and waste that these people carry with them, like a grudge, as part of their new-found leisure, is just a little depressing: retired farmers, mill hands, and their descendants, they are now anchored to the despoilment of their own class dignities by the hardware of the turnkey and the visible chimeras of the TV glimmering beyond the office alcove, where their seamy living quarters begin. The men wear sport shirts and pants; the women dress in sloppy joes and middy blouses, or little housedresses. It's as if their presently *lumpen* state of undress was intended to prepare one for the *deshabille* of the rooms: neutral-toned carpets, blonde wood furniture with pipe-stem legs, cigarette burns on the tables, never a desk or a headboard, but a TV, of course, and a *haut parleur* high against the wall (from which emanates hi-fi noises) and a little supported plank with a bench underneath which is called a dressing-table, and a thin cotton counterpane in light colors, which is tricked with runs and tiny holes, and everything in the bathroom wrapped in sanitary tissues. Usually, such places supply you with complimentary pieces of unlatherable soap, sanitary napkins, shoeshine rags, and copies of *Guideposts*, and they give off such a strong odor of ammonia that it would seem as if a pair of extremely hardy lovemakers had just completed a lengthy tryst. The motel keeper breathes asthmatically and says: "Cleaning woman has just left. Why don't you try the air conditioner?" Or, if it happens not to work: "Some people don't like the traffic, so we keep the shades down." Then he will start quoting prices: eight dollars a day, fifty by the week, and a ten per cent discount if you're in town on business: "And, of course, use the pool all you like."

But it's never that much of a sales pitch because, for one thing, the ruthless movement of traffic on the road outside means that just as soon as you depart, somebody else is bound to pop up and, for another, because there's something on the TV he would much rather enjoy watching, or there's the little patch of lemon shrub to tend, or there are dogs to be scolded. Sometimes there are pairs or even trios of tiny Pekinese-type dogs barking at one's cuffs throughout the initial inspection tour and, afterwards, when one comes outside in the bright hot sun, there is just the faintest whiff of dog turd or sewage which, apparently, no amount of sanitary tissue and disinfectant can effectively banish.

When I was a graduate student at Stanford at about the time of Dwight Eisenhower's second heart attack, I used to stay at such places quite often, and I usually could afford to. I remember one completely plasticized set of units outside Sacramento: it was one of those motor courts which displayed medallions from various state-touring associations attesting to its cleanliness and comfort, but, in truth, it was so ruthlessly clean that it was rather discomforting. I slept on a hard pallet in an iced room and felt very much like a slab of left-over sandwich meat that just had been placed inside the refrigerator for the night. Over pancakes and coffee at breakfast the next morning, I studied my placemat and coached myself on all the historic events which had taken place in the immediate vicinity; and when my order of pork sausage was late in delivery, I let the hot cakes grow cold and tried to guess the names of the various flowers on the little paper sugar bags. But the slight stench of what I took to be sewage was pervasive; it took the edge off my appetite. At last, my blonde plasticized waitress appeared in black dacron rather like a starched negligee and handed me the check. "I'm curious," I said. "Can you tell me what that odor is?"

"Oh that," she smiled in a voice that was purest Iowa: "That's just pig shit. *Haven't you ever smelled pig shit?*" And she was back a minute later with my order of cold sausage and a splash of hot black coffee.

If one is an academic remittance man supplemented by a graduate fellowship, eight to ten dollars a day may be just about right, but when one is being supported only by a modest publishers' advance, he tries to lodge on three to four dollars a day. As I headed out along the Imperial Highway through the industrial districts of South LA, I thought I should try to concentrate as many hours of every day as I could in meeting people and talking with them, and that seemed to indicate that I should look for a motel in the Negro district of town.

The road I took rushes along right through the center of the Watts battle zone. Even a year after the burnings, the air was fine with ash and cinders. The Negro men still stood out on the hot streets with their bottles inside paper bags, and the gutters were splashed with so many puddles of oil from old leaking cars that, under bright sun, with the radio giving off the casualty reports from Vietnam, it seemed almost as if the bloodletting had only just been halted. The streets were quiet. A little too quiet, perhaps, considering the fact that there were so many people standing about. And though I had read that very morning in the LA *Times* about all the various self-help and rebuilding operations that were under way, there were blocks which resembled the back lot at the old Fox Studios when the sets are being struck: lots piled high with a rubble of bricks and wood and charred retaining walls everywhere; danger signs poking out of piles of smoke-encrusted mattress ticking. In one residential area, hundreds of black children were playing among these newly created vest-pocket rubble heaps, and with the place thick with truck traffic, they would race recklessly across the wide avenue to another heap as if the score between them and the white man could be finally settled by bringing a liability suit against him. The morning news had announced the shooting of James Meredith, and I wondered what the various idlers, some of whom had transistor radios, were making of all that, but was too intimidated to inquire. It just seemed fair to assume that Vietnam, Meredith's shooting—they were all viewed as part of the same conspiracy against the black man. Then, somewhere in Willowbrook, I came upon my first motel, a greenish low building of stripped-down cinder block with a sign in front on which only the word "Gardens" was still legible. Painted onto the walls, however, was the motto: "Watts 66." And then another scribble: "Horse Shit!" I parked the car and was about to look for the renting office when a large white policeman pulled his motorcycle up along the traffic side of my car: "Can I help you, sir?"

I said: "I don't think so," as under his anxious gaze, I reluctantly locked the car door.

But he was persistent: "Is there," he asked, after another glance at my preposterous size alongside the little red car, "anything you would particularly like around here?"

Deciding not to be coy, I told him I was just going to book a room at *that* motel.

"What motel?" he asked, looking very puzzled.

I pointed to the long green row of little blockhouses.

"You won't find what you're looking for over there, mister."

"I just don't see how that's any of your business," I said, because I had read all about the late Chief Parker's police, and I wasn't going to let any of them tell me what to do. But the officer remained remarkably calm. He had a crewcut and a smooth face that was just a little pink, and his eyes were large and comfortable in their glance at me. He wore a white crash helmet, but he removed it presently to scratch his head, and when he put it back on again and smiled at me, he seemed much less intimidating, almost boyish in fact. Meanwhile, I could see that we had attracted a crowd of loiterers. Coming around to my side of the car, he asked: "Would you mind telling me your name?"

"Well, Richard," he said when I had told him, "I guess you're a stranger here because, you see, that isn't a motel. It's a housing project. You know. For the poor people? I just thought you might like to know. If you're looking for a motel, there are plenty back that way," pointing off in the direction of downtown LA from which I had come, "or that way," pointing toward the south: "But just so you won't get the wrong idea, I would like you to understand that *this is definitely a housing project.*" He shook my hand and said: "Have a nice visit," and he strutted away like a cowboy in a Western face-off.

Never mind my embarrassment, if that was a housing project I was now completely disoriented. There weren't more than eight tiny units with little boxy windows and a wooden stoop in front, flat roofs, no trees anywhere. It looked just the way motels used to look before affluence made all distinctions meaningless. As I walked slowly back to the driver's side of the car, wondering what the onlookers had made of the little transaction, I heard the officer blast off on his cycle while I leaned over with my key to unlock the door. Somebody had scratched a drawing of a penis into the tomato-red glaze with a sharp metal object. Looking up, I saw a Negro man smiling at me.

"Kids," he said. "They do those things all the time."

"Did you see them?" I asked.

"Yeah," he said. "I saw them." But that was all he said. After a moment, I got back into the car and drove on.

It wasn't long before another place popped into view, but this time I hesitated, seeing the sign but no building. All that I could see, in fact, was a shabby little private house with a sign nailed to a palm: "MOTEL UNITS, $12 weekly." But there were so many fewer idlers on this particular block that I parked the car and started up toward the stoop. Then a sign with another arrow appeared, directing me toward the back yard.

The yard was blacktopped and had a tall hurricane fence surrounding it. In the center of the yard, a fat orange tabby cat glared at me like a piece of porcelain garden statuary. Ahead of me now was a low building with a flat roof and four red doors cut into it, each about ten feet apart. One of these doors was half ajar. As I came closer I heard the whirring of a vacuum cleaner. I looked for a sign directing me toward the office, but there didn't seem to be any. I started toward the open door.

As if on signal, the whirring of the vacuum stopped and a woman's head appeared, small and dark, with hair the color of dust. She said: "I told my husband you'd be getting here."

"I'm looking for a room," I said, startled by her greeting.

The woman laughed as she stepped out into the sun: "You don't see that many white faces around here. I thought you were from the County."

"I'm afraid not," I told her, before inquiring once again about a room.

"I'm sorry," she shrugged, "we're all rented."

I said, "I'm sorry."

"Yes," she said, "I am too because, you know, we have a couple of men who the State is paying for living here and I would like very much to get rid of them. That's why I was hoping you were from the Welfare, but you say you're not. You say you just want a room. Well okay, if that's what you say you want. I just wish I could help you. I've asked them to move those bums some place else so I can get decent people to move in here, but they say there just isn't any place else. Today they said they'd come over and take a look, only they haven't been here yet and I have to take my husband over to the VA hospital in a little while.

"That's the way it is," the woman said. "We always seem to be missing each other. I'll come back and they'll have been here, and then what? I'll have to get them back here again."

I started to turn away but she said, "It's not that I like chasing people out of my place, but some people just don't know how to behave sometimes. They drink in the rooms and they bring their women here, and I just don't like any of that and it disturbs my husband. Personally, I don't mind it that much, but if it disturbs my husband then I have to do something about it, don't I?"

She was walking beside me as I went back out toward the car. When I opened the door she said: "You're only a few blocks from Compton. You ought to be able to find a place there."

"Are there many places?" I asked.

The woman shrugged: "I wouldn't know. I never go there if I can help it," and she waved good-bye to me as I got back into the car and drove off. It was another twenty blocks before I was sure I was in Compton, and then it was only because I got stopped by a policeman for having attempted a U-turn; on the side of his car was an emblem with the legend "HUB CITY" in the center of it.

. . .

"You know what it's like?" Rina Edwards said. "Do you have even the slightest idea?" Each time that she spoke, her voice grew a little huskier, until she finally seemed to be on the verge of shouting: "He's been like this all winter long. I just think he's scared . . . afraid to move outside that front door.

"Well, I won't even say that I blame him," she continued. "He was running on those streets with all the others. He tells people he wasn't because he's so scared, but I know differently. Would you believe it?" she added, abruptly, "The night we got together again, everything around here was burning sky high. He came back and there was blood all over his trousers. I didn't ask any questions. You better get yourself inside, boy, I said. Him wanting me to believe that it all happened by accident . . . well, I could see right through him with that kind of stuff. He was in the Thrifty Drug when the police came. One of his legs got slashed going out the window. Then the policeman shot at him. You could see the little bullet hole in his slacks. That bullet went in the front of his thigh and out the back way again. He's just lucky he's so meaty it didn't smash any bones. Look at him," Rina smiled. "He was damn near caught red-handed and all he's got to show for it is that case of Scotch whiskey which he doesn't even drink. He almost got himself killed for a case of Hankey Bannister Scotch whiskey. You want some, I'll give you some. He won't like that one bit. Just look at him."

The subject of this narrative was a wiry, thin-faced Negro male with high cheek bones. Probably the man was in his late thirties, for there was a slight silvering among the close hairs on his temples, yet he might have been younger or even older by as much as half a decade. There was something that tentative, indefinite, about his total appearance. Throughout the woman's harangue, this man had listened with a grave, somewhat bored expression on his face, as if all three of us had been gossiping about a fourth person whom he hardly knew. Sometimes he would let his lids close over his eyes, casting his face up toward the dusty light streaming in through the only window, so that his lips seemed as grey as slate. He kept his hands, meanwhile, folded across the front of his frayed white T shirt, and they were large, dark, and well-formed. Encased in stiff blue jeans, one of his thick legs was stretched out awkwardly and the other rested across it slantwise, with the loafered foot jammed against the arm of a shabby wing chair. The back of that same chair stood more than a foot above his head. Dwarfed within such a frame, he yawned and stretched out his arms, the small of his back resting against a pillow, his crossed leg like a discarded crutch. Then he folded his arms once again across his chest.

"If you're so sleepy, don't just sit there. Go on to bed," the woman said, but I wished she would call him by name, for we hadn't been introduced. In fact, the fellow had hardly taken any notice of me when she had led me into the room, talking away. Throughout, he just kept staring at the woman, who was small, pretty, blacker than he was, and had large almond-shaped eyes. It wasn't as if the man was angry at Rina for talking out of turn to a white stranger like myself, but as if he had heard it all before in the presence of scores of other white intruders—social workers, the local ministers, or perhaps some of the neighbors—as if Rina was always bringing around people whom she presumed she could trust to gossip to about him. "I don't have any hope of making him see eye-to-eye with me," Rina admitted.

The man said: "Don't you bother about what she says. She only thinks she knows what happened. Actually, she don't know what she's talking about."

"I know more than you think," Rina fired back at him. But she immediately drew herself back from that posture of defiance. Now there was even a drabness, a flatness to her voice: "That night he come back, we were all frightened to death. You think you were the only ones afraid? I was terrified. The children were crying. My oldest was South for the summer at momma's. I had the young ones. How did we know what was going to happen? I put my kids to bed as soon as it was dark, and then I stayed with them in their room with all the lights turned out. We slept on the floor that night because we didn't want to be near the windows. Well, if you remember, it was awful hot and musty outside. With the windows open, we could smell the smoke from down on Wilmington where they burned out Manny's. All kinds of talking was in the air. My neighbors said some of those rednecks in Paramount were going to come in here and shoot the place up to get even. You just don't know how helpless we felt, but there was no place we could go. If you walked out on the streets after curfew, you were dead. Seemed like every couple of minutes they'd be shooting at somebody and then a whole army would come marching through here, trucks, sirens, you name it. Well, when *he* came, I thought he meant to bring the National Guards right down on top of us and they would want to search this place from top to bottom. I wasn't taking any chances, but there he was and what could I do? As I say, they were shooting just about everybody in sight but he got over the back fence to our kitchen door. 'Rina,' he's calling, 'Rina, do you hear me?' And when that didn't do any good, he nearly frightened my little girl to death because he started yelling: 'Charmayne . . . Charmayne . . .'

41

which is the name of my oldest but she was with my momma in Arkansas. I guess he figured Charmayne would still have a soft spot for him even if I didn't.

"Well," the woman continued, more briskly, trying to smile, "I guess I should have known better but I just couldn't shut the door that way on their daddy. I couldn't let Baxter stand out there all night, so I hushed the children because they were all wide awake by now, and went around and let him in the back way. It was a good thing I did, because just then Lenny from next door sticks her head out the window: 'Rina, you better make up your mind real quick about that boy because there's a police car coming down the street.'

"Baxter was wearing white clam diggers and a T shirt just like he is now and when I opened the door and saw him, with that case of whiskey in his arms, all covered with his own blood, I don't know, for some reason I was reminded of that interne at the General Hospital when I gave birth to Rosalee and they couldn't stop the bleeding. He had that same funny surprised look on his face, except that this other man was Mexican. 'I don't want to hear any questions . . . not a thing, you hear?' That's the way he spoke. He pushed right past me. Then he said: 'Shut that door, woman,' and when I saw him again he was crouching down there on the kitchen floor, holding those legs and breathing heavy. He's been here ever since. At first I wanted him to get rid of all that whiskey, but he told me nothing doing. I gave him some hot milk, bandaged him

42

up, and I carried him a pillow and told him he could sleep on the floor. Well, the leg didn't heal and Baxter turned out to be afraid of mice, so I finally gave him that room— the room I am going to rent to you—*just as soon as Baxter takes his whiskey and gets out of here.*

"*Do you hear me, Baxter?*"

Rina had raised her voice again because he seemed to be dropping off to sleep. Then she added, for my benefit, "To tell you the God's honest truth, I just wish there was some place else he could go, some place he could get work because he would find a place of his own. Now all he does is hang around with those street people talking a lot of foolish talk.

"*I said foolish,*" she added, loudly, although Baxter still didn't seem as if he was about to interrupt her. Then she added: "What's the difference? What's the use? Who cares?"

"You just keep spilling out your heart," Baxter said. "There ain't nobody really cares."

It was only the second time he had spoken, and even though he was being rude, it forced Rina to smile: "You see what I mean?"

A moment later her voice was quietly emphatic: "Please be nice, Baxter. This man isn't bothering you. He came here to see the room."

Baxter said: "My room!"

"You got no call on it," Rina said. "This man is my guest."

"Welcome, guest!" Baxter waved a hand in the air expansively. "Welcome to Compton, California, a suburb of Watts."

"We live in Willowbrook," Rina corrected him.

"Call it what you like, it's still Watts," Baxter said. "Just read any newspaper." He turned my way: "Would you believe it, she thinks all you got to do is move out of Central Avenue and you're like all the rest of those white folks up there in the Palos Verdes Estates. Horseshit! Watts," he added with considerable drama again, "is everywhere that black men are living like scarecrows. It's Pacoima. It's West Adams. It's Oakland. It's Vietnam. Besides, I don't think it matters where you live. It's who you living with."

"It isn't at all like that," Rina insisted. "There's a lot to be said for Willowbrook."

"And Compton too," Baxter leered.

Rina said: "I suppose you think *that's just like Watts.*"

It was difficult to know which of their assertions was the more correct. In fact, that little white paint-flaked bungalow lay beneath a skeletal jacaranda tree, blooming all lavender behind a row of stores, near where the Southern Pacific tracks cross Rosecrantz into Compton, but people here sent their children to Compton schools. In fact, Rina Edwards had come to this portion of Willowbrook from the Central Avenue district in Watts for precisely that reason; and she had come to Central Avenue, in turn, from Eldorado, Arkansas, in the winter of 1950. Since her arrival in Southern California, Rina had been married and divorced once, and married and separated a second time, bearing three children. For years her oldest girl had lived with her grandmother in Arkansas, but now Rina had all three of them with her and felt more independent than ever before. After nearly a decade on public assistance, she had found work in a roadside rest inside Compton, where I had met her, and she was able to rent this five-room bungalow in Willowbrook, hoping shortly to pick herself up and, with the help of Welfare, find a larger place inside city limits.

My involvement with Rina began with a dispute over an order at the roadside rest. On that first day in Compton, I had stopped at the stand and asked for a hamburger and a root beer. Seeing Rina start to spread mayonnaise on my hamburger, I said: "Please don't," but my expression must have betrayed a rather strong twinge of disgust because she said: "I'm sorry, mister, that's what we're supposed to do. They call it California style.

"You don't want any fresh tomato and pickle on it?" she inquired a moment later, after dropping another burger on the grill.

Again I shook my head emphatically no.

Rina made the logical conclusion: I was not a Californian. She handed me the plain hamburger on a sesame seed bun and then pushed the bowls of chopped onion and tomato catsup toward my plate. But when I asked for mustard, it was her turn to take offense. She fetched it for me with a look of disgust, asking: "Are you German?"

I said I was not, and asked why she thought I might be. Rina said that her next-door neighbor had married a German girl, and they used a lot of mustard on their food. She stared at me, as if waiting for me to explain what I was and what I was doing here. I hesitated. The only trouble was there wasn't any other business in the place and after going to scrape off her griddle Rina returned: "Just passing through?"

I explained that I was planning to be in Compton for about a month, and that, as a matter of fact, I was even now looking for a place to stay.

"Plenty of nice motels out on the Long Beach Road," Rina said.

I told her that I was on a very limited budget and wanted to be "nearer to things."

Rina asked, "What things?"

"I just would like to be with people," I said.

Rina frowned, but she offered no suggestions, and I was still hesitant to make a specific request that she recommend a place. Two hours later, when I passed the stand again after another futile search for reasonably priced accommodations, I stopped by for a sip of cold root beer. Rina immediately dismissed her customer and came to where I was standing: "Find anything?"

When I reported that I still hadn't, her face seemed to brighten. She asked, "Just what kind of place you looking for?" And when I told her that I wanted some place cheap that would be "nearer to things," Rina said, "I have a place. I'll let you look at it, if you like.

"I'll tell you what," Rina hurried past her own initial invitation so I hardly had the chance to voice my disapproval, "in five minutes I'm relieved. I don't own a car. If you drive me home I'll show you the place. It isn't much

but it's right in the thick of things. If you like it, I can let
you have it cheap. We won't get in your way. I promise."

"Who are we?" I asked.

"My kids . . . my family . . . you know."

Bus service in that part of Los Angeles is always a problem, so I decided that even if Rina's place might not be
suitable, the least I could do was to be obliging enough to
give her a lift home. Fifteen minutes later, when we
walked out past her smirking replacement toward the
Volkswagen, she suddenly asked: "How much do you think
you would be willing to pay?" I confessed I didn't know.
She shrugged her shoulders and got into the front seat with
me. As we moved out of the parking lot and turned onto
Compton Boulevard, she added: "There's somebody in the
room right now. He'll be leaving."

"Who might that be?" I asked. Rina didn't answer.

"Look," I said then, "I wouldn't want to have you chase
anybody out for my sake."

"It's all right," she said. "He's just my husband."

And that, terribly enough, was all she would say in ex-
planation until I had parked the car in her alleyway and
had come around to where she was standing by the back
door. "About that man I told you about," Rina told me
then, "my husband, he's harmless. He just says a lot of
things to hear himself talk. Don't listen to any of that."

The trouble with such warnings is that they always come
too late. If she had said anything about that back at the
hamburger stand, I would have mustered up an appropriate
excuse for not wanting to see the room, and dropped her

on her front stoop. Now how could I turn back? I said: "I understand," although it must have been clear from my expression that I really didn't, and then I stood alongside Rina as she let me through her back hall. Clearly, she was intent upon showing off her place, whether I took the room or not, and it was probably just as well that I followed around after her.

Rina led me into her kitchen first to show me the washing machine that was "like new," which she had purchased only the month before at Julie's on Rosecrantz. "It's a Maytag," she chattered. "The German lady next door says that means May Day."

But we were now admiring the pair of redwood bunk beds in the children's room; she had purchased them from Manny's on Wilmington "just a few days before they burned him out." I noticed a Stanford pennant stuck to one wall. "One of my kids found that," Rina explained. "It's just a joke." And when it seemed as if I hadn't caught on, she added: "You know. *Smile.*"

Then she showed me the ample double bed in her room and, with another "smile," quickly shut the door on it so that I might not get the wrong idea ("smile") before she took me across the corridor to the barely opened door of the guest room, the room I surmised she was proposing to rent to me. Rina poked open the door and peered inside. "He must be in the parlor," she said. "You can look around in here all you like."

But there wasn't that much to look at. It was just a narrow musty room reeking of strong disinfectant. Against one wall was a cot with a khaki cotton army blanket stretched across the bare mattress. A space as wide as the rag mat that covered it separated this from a plain wooden tool table which was also quite bare, and just a trifle dusty. Against one corner of that table was clamped a tiny metal vise. There was an elbow joint of copper pipe lying on the table, a metal tool box, and an unopened roll of black friction tape. There were also two books: An S&H Green Stamps catalogue and a paperback edition of *The Carpetbaggers*. Stacked in the farthest corner were a pile of thin dun-colored brochures. "He said he wanted to take a home study course," Rina explained, "so I got him those."

"It's like a lot of things," she added. "They never worked out."

But *they*, in this case, upon closer inspection, proved to be an entire set of U.S. Army field manuals for the operation and maintenance of various types of communications equipment: field telephones, walkie-talkies, vehicular radios, battery-pack operated radios. As I was shuffling through the pile, somebody coughed on the other side of the wall. I said: "These seem a little out of date."

"On the Welfare," Rina said, "it was the best I could do." She lifted the pile out of my hands and placed them back in their corner. Then she led me out of the room and closed the door. We were standing quite close to one another now in her narrow corridor. Rina said: "I guess you won't be wanting the place, after all."

"I guess not," I told her. "But I'd like to thank you for your trouble."

49

"You don't have to thank me for anything," Rina said. She started to walk toward the front parlor. Then we saw Baxter. "Strike me dead," Rina said, but she insisted that I come in with her, and that was when she had started to tell me about what had happened: "You know what it's like? Do you even have the slightest idea?"

Now, although it was nearly half an hour since Baxter and I were brought together, it seemed like I had been with them the whole day. The room was becoming quite close. Rina was speaking again, her hands clamped against her narrow, childlike hips: "A man hasn't worked in two years. . . . Do you know what it's like for him? Do you have even the slightest idea?"

Outside, a gang of men began to hammer at some railroad ties so loudly that I couldn't hear the rest of what she was saying, but I heard Baxter's reply: "Take it easy, baby." And then I heard Rina say: "What I got to be so easy about?"

A helicopter throbbed overhead. Within the tiny unfurnished parlor I sat against the wall on a strip of rattan carpeting. Between me and Baxter in the wing chair Rina stood, clad in black pedal pushers and a sleeveless white blouse. Her coarse dark hair was done up in an elegant French bun. The gang stopped their hammering. Rina said, "It wasn't as if he ever had any real jobs out here. What did you ever do, Baxter? Still, if you would ask me, I can't say that I would blame you for some of your ideas. I just don't see what good they going to do. I keep telling him next time they will shoot to kill."

Once again, Baxter didn't even seem to be listening. I said, "I don't think there's going to be a next time."

"Get us some beer," Baxter said.

Rina said: "Get it yourself!" But she went toward the kitchen and fetched some for me and, of course, she brought a bottle to Baxter. "Well," Rina said then, "if you not going to take the room, there ain't too much we can talk about." She glanced at her husband: "You real lucky Baxter." Then she added, "If you don't want the room, drink up and come back another day. My kids ought to be back soon and I got a lot to do."

Then Baxter said, "You heard her. She's got a lot to do. You come back here another day and maybe you'll have better luck."

I asked Baxter what he meant by that, but he just smiled, and neither one budged from where they were to show me out the door. But, as I stood in the alleyway alongside my car, I heard Baxter again: "You ought to know better. That man wouldn't live in a place like this."

"What's wrong with this place?"

"Nothing wrong," Baxter said, "only I guess you stuck with me a good while longer."

I don't know whether Rina slapped Baxter then, or Baxter slapped Rina, but I can't forget hearing Rina's voice: "Get away from me Baxter. Get away you hear. You just get away from me, Baxter. Just leave me alone!"

As I backed out of the driveway, a crowd of their neighbors had gathered, and I had to blow my horn frantically for them to part so that I could make my way through.

51

CHAPTER III

A HOUSE AWAY FROM HOME

I didn't see Rina again for another week. By then, I was safely installed in a tiny shabby motel room in Willowbrook. The Indian Sycamore Lodge was a small low blockhouse of poured concrete faced with brick and redwood and built around a tiny court which you entered through a redwood gate screened on the inside with bamboo. To the right was the apartment of Noni and her husband, Blake, the managers, who lived cramped together in five small rooms with their six children, all under ten; beyond this, and joined to it, was the wing of motel units, about twelve in all. At five dollars a night, all were invited to "Be our guest," as the sign on the roof advertised; after my first few nights there I discovered that not only was I the only white person on the premises, but I was also the only person who spent the whole night.

The Indian Sycamore was a successful business venture precisely because few of its guests ever stayed longer than three hours, for which Noni was instructed to charge a mere $3.50; and some came and went in less than an hour. Although this constant traffic of shack jobs, prostitutes and their clients, unfaithful husbands and their girlfriends, sailors on leave, prosperous white businessmen and their Negro mistresses, spiffy black hustlers and dyed-blonde housewives, kept Noni up half the night registering them for rooms, changing linens, and mopping bathroom floors, it produced what must have been a substantial profit for the owner, a certain white businessman named Mr. Zorax, who happened to live in Pasadena. Moreover, Noni and her clients were always discreet. I doubt if many of the pensioners—white or black—who lived in the frame houses to all sides of us, ever knew just what was going on at the Indian Sycamore. As the cars drove up, often in broad daylight or early dusk onto the tiny ramplike street which led into the entrance of the Indian Sycamore, they would be seated on their porches, staring up at the smoggy sky overhead, or perhaps glancing down at a newspaper across their laps.

In fact, I must confess that even I was not aware of the intensive use to which the Indian Sycamore was being put by Southern California's erotic community until the morning that I had to stay in and type some notes. It was one of those hazy hot Southern California June days, and I had the door open, facing the courtyard as I typed. Outside, Noni was moving from room to room with her little shopping cart of mops and rags and fresh linens imitating her favorite vocalist, Nancy Wilson: *"How glad . . . I am . . ."* But she was continually interrupted. Car after car pulled up, the driver emerging to haggle with her over the price of a room "for just a few hours." "You going to be alone?" Noni would say, and the man would tell her that he was expecting somebody. They would then settle on the $3.50 "paid in advance," and Noni would have to go to the office to make up a registration card and copy down the license plates. "Remember," she would say, "more than three hours and I got to charge you the full rate."

But that morning nobody seemed to stay more than one hour. As one lone Negro soldier later put it to me, "I'm just going to drop a little load and scram on out of here." But that was another day, another time. This particular morning, as I sat at my little desk, the dull concatenation of cars driving in and out with doors swinging open and slamming shut made it seem as if I were writing alongside a concourse of pneumatic drills. One man said to Noni, "I'll just be a little while. I just want to be by myself a little while." And, sure enough, he did what he had to do and left, half an hour later, minus $3.50. Later, another inquired: "Are there any girls here? *You know what I mean, don't you, girls?*"

"Oh I know what you mean," Noni told him (and I imagined that delicious glow of amusement usurping the usually somber cast of her expression), "but I can't help you, mister. I'm sorry. I can't help you. I rent rooms here, that's all. What you put in those rooms is your business, but I can't help you. You'll just have to do that on your own."

That man didn't take the room, although one other single woman did, used it for ten minutes, emerged insisting that she hadn't soiled any of the sheets—and could she possibly get a partial refund? But most of Noni's tenants were well provided with companions. They would drive up in separate cars and come together at the rental office. Or they would stroll in casually from the street, as if they had come to the Sycamore by foot, and inquire with a mock-informality about the possibilities of a room for a couple of hours "because we want to get cleaned up and change our clothes." But none of these passers-by ever seemed to be carrying suitcases with them, and some were clearly using pseudonyms on the registration cards, for there was a predominance of Smiths and Browns and Joneses and even, quite originally, one Negro man who insisted his name was Samuel Yorty.

Noni accepted everybody for what they said they were, and collected her $3.50. The only time I heard her complain was when two couples wanted to rent one room for "a little party." "Uh . . . uh . . . The last time that happened," Noni told them stubbornly, "the bed broke and we had to get another. I couldn't rent the room for a week. It just wasn't worth it." Presently, she had this foursome agreeing to take turns (one couple waited in the car while the other was inside) at no extra charge and, when they had gone about their business, I heard her exclaim: "Goddamn. I ain't seen the likes of it."

But, for the most part that morning, Noni kept herself in check, making none but the most businesslike comments except when a Mexican couple in work clothes drove up in a battered Plymouth with a small, coughing baby in their arms. Noni had to reluctantly turn them away because there weren't any rooms, but she said, "Come back in an hour," and she volunteered to warm some milk for the baby. Then a fat white man and a little Negro teen-ager with purple pop-art glasses emerged from one of the rooms and Noni said: "You just go inside and wait a second. I have to clean up." But when the couple asked what the cost of the rooms would be and they were told five dollars, the man grunted, "Too much," and pushed his wife toward the car again.

I don't know how much business Noni actually conducted between, say, 8:30 in the morning and 2 that afternoon (when I went out for lunch), but I was disappointed later when she told me she didn't work on commissions because, if she had, she would have done quite well. There wasn't an empty room in the place all that day for longer than fifteen minutes at a stretch, and the courtyard was drenched with the sleazy sexual innuendo. My own room happened to be close to dead center within that block of motel units, so I could hear the various couples whispering together through the plasterboard walls: "No baby no . . .

*Not that way . . . I can't help myself . . . No . . . Oh please
baby please now baby please. . . ."*

It was a trifle embarrassing, even obscene, to be eavesdropping, even though it was perfectly unintentional, but I
justified my presence there by insisting that I had to do the
work that morning. And, after all, I argued with myself, I
had been given to understand that I was renting a motel
room, not space in an *estaminet,* and for my five dollars I
had as much right to be there as anybody else. It was just
too bad if all these other couples couldn't keep their lovemaking to an appropriately inaudible whisper; I had my
work to do and I wasn't going to budge. Besides, didn't
they have work to do somewhere . . . some place?

I told myself somewhat unconvincingly that it all just
sounded too much like a put-up job—as if all those flashy
Negro women in their purple sunglasses and white flannel
skirts were being paid to moan and chatter and screech
"baby, baby" while their men labored away at them heav-
ily, making the concrete blocks tremble and the bed springs
squeak. It just wasn't possible that there was that much
real passion left in the world on such a hot smoggy day in
an unairconditioned room. All of it had to be fake, part of
the well-known LA art of the spurious, and, if that was so,
I wasn't eavesdropping after all.

And, needless to say, I was only deceiving myself because,
like it or not, I had been eavesdropping, and that was about
all that one could say for such behavior.

But what to do? Gathering my notes together, I headed

for the door. Just as I'd closed it shut behind me, Noni appeared: "You don't lock it? You mustn't take chances like that. Around here people will steal anything. Don't you know how to lock that door?"

Noni is a tall, brown, lean woman with big hands, big feet, large eyes and ears; she wears her long black hair in braids. There is almost something handsome about her haggard, imposing style of homeliness, quite manly, but quite feminine at the same time. Noni, in fact, resembles an Indian brave; in profile she would look very much like the chief on the Indian nickel (which jibes with what she told me, much later, about being part Cherokee), but the even temper, the strong shrewd smile, the way she had of taking your measure with those big eyes and then dropping you again, just like that, that was largely Southern Negro.

At first, I felt rather intimidated in Noni's presence, especially when I realized that she might have rented my room at a much greater profit to her transients. As a consequence, I studiously avoided her, coming and going with only a nod. But that morning, after she had challenged me for not locking my door, I was even more perplexed than usual. "What's the matter?" she asked. "If you don't know how to lock the door I'll have to show you."

She took me by the wrist, leading me back over to the door. "Here," she explained, twisting the imitation brass handle before pushing it in, "you turn it this way and then you push like that at the same time and it's locked. See! Isn't that simple? You think you can remember?"

"I'll remember," I said.

"And if you're afraid of losing the key, leave it with me and I'll fetch it for you whenever you come back."

"Thank you."

"You sure you understand?"

"Yes, Mrs. . . ."

"You call me Noni," she smiled. "Most people around here do."

"Well, look, Noni," I said, "I'm sorry I put you to all that trouble," because I realized then that she had been maintaining a kind of silent vigil over my valuables, along with all her other chores, "I really am sorry," fumbling with the key in the lock once again because I remembered that I had left a book in my room. But when I stepped outside again and shut the door, once more I forgot to twist the lock.

Again, Noni stood in the courtyard, smiling: "I ought to let you get robbed. Then maybe you will learn a little lesson."

"I'm sorry," I said, a third time, as I went to lock the door. Noni said, "I guess you're not used to living with these kind of people."

"I guess not . . ."

"Look," I added, "would it suit you better if I found another place? I mean, I gather you could do much better if you had the room to rent on an hourly basis."

Noni said, "I'm satisfied if you are."

"I was just thinking . . ."

"Don't," she interrupted me. "Just don't bring any girls

59

in here," she winked, "and let's not hear any more about you moving out."

. . .

That afternoon, I tried to take lunch in a Compton tavern less than a block away. The place advertised Michelob on tap, and I was extremely thirsty.

It was a small dark place with a damp smell to it. Above the bar was the customary TV, and there was a large Anheuser Busch clock nestled among the glasses and the whiskey bottles. About four white men had their backs to me when I entered. The Dodger game was blaring away. When I took my stool, the bartender, a fat man with one ear slightly cauliflowered, gasped, "Hot out there."

"I'll have a Michelob," I told him.

"All out."

"Well then I'll take what you've got."

"Hamms or Coors?"

"Hamms."

"I'll just have to see if I've got any," he smiled.

The noises from the television grew louder. It seemed as if the crowd was shouting angrily. I remembered that the Dodgers were in San Francisco. "Who's winning?" I asked, as the bartender slid a bottle of Coors in front of me and took a quarter off my pile of change.

A thin-faced man with sandy hair and a deep brown sash of wrinkled flesh around his neck turned my way, pointing with his glass in hand up toward the screen. By now, the booing of the crowd was at a feverish pitch. I recognized the squat figure of Dodger catcher John Roseboro at the plate. Only a week before, he had brawled with Giant star Juan Marichal. Swinging his bat around to limber himself, Roseboro was trying to appear unconcerned, but the booing grew louder still and there were now pieces of paper dropping all around him from the grandstands. Since Roseboro was a Compton resident, I felt sure that my bar companions would have something to say about this, and they did. Just then, the booing drowned out the voice of the announcer, and the man with the wrinkled neck said, "Those niggers are really after that nigger . . .

"You just watch," he said, "those niggers are really going to get themselves that nigger."

By now, the television pandemonium was such that it was spurring the fellow on. In the sanctity of his all-white bar he really let loose: "Goddamn niggers. You want to see a scared one, just look up there at that TV. Just take a look at that scared nigger."

The other men had started to laugh uncomfortably, but the man at the end of the bar with the sandy hair had no inhibitions. He kept on: "Those San Francisco niggers are really going to get that nigger. You wait and see. They'll be getting that Compton nigger. It will serve him right."

He was staring at me fiercely, as if to gauge the extent of my sympathies. "Take it easy, Ned," the fat bartender said cautiously. But the man just shrugged him off and swigged more beer. "I used to live in this town," he said,

61

"until one day my kids come home with their school pictures and they were half nigger. How's a man supposed to have any pride living like that?"

And, saying that, he slumped down against the bar with his face in the cradle of his arms and seemed to go off to sleep. Just like that. One minute he was cursing, and the next he was folded up against the bar like a big baby. Then I heard him begin to sob. "You mustn't mind Ned," the bartender tried to explain, "he gets very emotional sometimes."

"Go fuck yourself, Barney," the sleeping man said. There was the sharp hard rap of a bat. Roseboro had lined out to the third baseman. "If that nigger only knew how to hit to the opposite field," the man said, raising his head as if in a daze. "He's got the power." And again he slumped against the bar.

I was pleased to get back to the Indian Sycamore, where Noni greeted me half an hour later. "Things have slackened off," she said. "I'm going to take a little nap. I think you'll be able to work now. The kids will be watching in case anybody comes in."

I looked over toward the office where her oldest boy, a child of ten in striped polo shirt and levis, was installed behind the little registration desk. "He's got studying to do," Noni said. "It won't hurt him to sit there. And he can keep an eye on the other kids too. I'm just dead tired. In a couple of hours my husband will be home, and it looks like I'm going to have a busy night. It's always busy this time of the year. I think it has something to do with the weather."

. . .

I stayed five weeks at the Indian Sycamore Lodge, perhaps an endurance (and certainly the longevity) record for the place, and Noni and I eventually became such good friends that she would invite me in to have a glass of cold pop or coffee with her. Once, I was even invited to a meager but tasty supper of hot beans with little pieces of meat in it, which Noni, her husband Blake, and the six children and I ate out of soup bowls with spoons. Noni was quick to apologize for the simplicity of the fare: "I don't cook here like I did in the South. I never have the time."

In those five weeks, I used the Indian Sycamore as my point of departure, base camp, and bivouac for my second painstaking exploration of Compton within four years. Sometimes this was conducted on foot, which marked me as someone rather odd even in Compton, but more often I went by car. On foot, I became familiar with all the little shacks with gardens along the Southern Pacific tracks, and, after a while, some of the old Mexican men and women who lived in them nodded to me when I passed, as if I was now a local. Occasionally, I would bump into Rina's Baxter, and he would stare at me sullenly while we exchanged hostile pleasantries; once, I passed Rina waiting for a bus, and she looked the other way. It wasn't until weeks later that I learned that Baxter was now getting a tiny income from a local training program of the Office of Economic Opportunity, and, according to my informant, Rina was also now hoping to get a divorce.

Walking, I also got to know Flores' Cafe, perhaps the only place in Compton where truly home-cooked meals were served, and I used to like to take lunch at their counter, trying to imitate the weathered old-timers who doused their steaks in *salsa* and drank steaming hot black coffee as if the insides of their mouths were made of galvanized tin. At Flores', one can eat a whole meal for under two dollars with a bottle of cold Mexican beer thrown in. Mrs. Flores and her daughter were also two of the most beautiful Mexican women I had ever seen: dark black hair and stark white skins (with little pink roses in the cheeks when they became flustered) and large deep eyes. I got to love their little homely cafe beside the railroad track, its noises, its smells, the boisterous Mexican students who sat for hours together arguing about soccer or pop music, the old men, Mr. Flores with his carefully patronish, *petit bourgeois* dignity—so inappropriate to California—and his son, a boy of perhaps thirteen who looked, for all the world, like a fat young prince of the Hapsburgs when he trundled about behind the counter after school in an apron, trying his best to help his mother.

Flores' became, in fact, a kind of link to the East for me. It was my way of forgetting about Baxter and Rina and sometimes even Noni. And perhaps I loved it most because it was also so unrepresentative of all the newness, garishness,

sleaziness, and slothfulness that was Southland. In Flores'
even the heat was muggier and less like a needle than in the
Southland at large; it was more like body warmth, I
thought, and so I came to eat nearly all my meals among
those lovely, formal people until, unused to that much
pungency, I had to live on porridge for two straight days.

Where else does one go in a place like Compton? One
never seems to be walking *to* anywhere. There just aren't
any such places to walk *toward*. Downtown, at the Compton Civic Center, lay a small viscous knot of stores and
cafés, public buildings, a tiny park with benches, a library,
but nobody ever seemed to be walking about in those
streets; even the mailboxes were equipped so that one could
drive past and let fly into their protruding snouts with a
letter. The place just wasn't meant to be walked *about* in.
I shall never forget my surprise when I came upon a group
of pickets outside the Bureau of Public Aid (Welfare).
They seemed odd, not because they were mostly hardy,
clean-looking former college kids in brightly colored sports
clothes, but because they were actually walking *about*, these
future bureaucrats, and with signs held above their heads.
"Pass them by," one shouted at me perfunctorily. What an
odd turn of phrase to use, considering the fact that I was
probably the only person who had actually passed by on
foot during that entire morning.

If people didn't walk much in Compton, a good many
did sit for long hours at a stretch, along the curbs, squint-
ing up at the sun, on their abbreviated porches, or in the
cafés, bars, laundromats, and even among the gas station

pumps. That's where I sometimes saw Baxter, gossiping among a group of Negro men in much the same desultory plight as he was. These grown men and women, all dressed in clean sport clothes, never seemed to have to be going anywhere except, perhaps, waiting for a lift back home again. They always seemed to be staring off into space, as if that lift were about to come at any moment. And if you asked such people directions, they were not usually helpful. "I'm not from Compton," they might say. Or perhaps just: "I don't live here."

The Compton neighborhood adjacent to the Indian Sycamore Lodge was, as I say, older and even somewhat shabbier than in some sections of Willowbrook itself, and much older and shabbier than most of the tract developments of Compton; I was surprised to learn later, from the Compton Master Plan, that this was an area scheduled for urban renewal. It was, after all, one of the few areas of town that truly had that "lived-in" look, and that is the very look which seems so intolerable to most Southern Californians. But not to the people who lived in that part of Compton. Not to the people who lived there. They were mostly old-timers who'd bought in years ago, had raised their children, and were now tending to their little shops and gardens, or they were young Negro couples with large families, renting until they could save enough to buy, or some were just loafing, pensioners so tied to class that they actually seemed to be dug in, rooted, like the wild gnarled things growing in their gardens. To everyone else I met, this section of town seemed to be deplorable, but the

police told me that the area was certainly not one of the
most criminally inclined districts, and if the homes were
shabby, they were not really dilapidated. Yet when I confessed to one middle-class Negro housewife that I was living near the Sycamore, she made a gagging noise before
turning away from me.

And she wasn't the only one. All the city functionaries
to whom I spoke later seemed to regard me as some peculiarly deviant species of social animal the moment I
mentioned the neighborhood in which I was staying. "It's
a funny part of town," was about the nicest way I heard it
expressed. One police employee was much more emphatic:
"What the hell are you doing down there?"

It was as if I'd walked in through Compton's back door,
unannounced. If that was the kind of man I was, how could
I possibly be trusted? Why didn't I go back out to one of
those motels on the Strip? A prominent lawyer asked me:
"Is it safe down there after dark?" His offices were located
less than three blocks away.

Just what was I after? If I was a real writer, I should be
living it up like a real writer at one of those motels on the
Strip. When I asked questions which revealed that, for an
outsider, I knew a great deal about Compton, I got fishy
stares. Just why were these homeowners so distrustful of a
person like me? It surely had nothing to do with the proposed urban renewal, for most people seemed surprised to
learn that it was even planned. I could understand that
someone like Noni needed to be circumspect to protect her
trade, but why, when I went down the block one afternoon

to a nearby hotel (which rented almost exclusively to single men) to buy some postage stamps, did the man behind the counter ask: "What you been hanging around for, mister?"

The gun-slinger comes to town, and word gets around from saloonkeeper to desk clerk to local cattle baron. But this was Compton, California, in the summer of 1966, not Dodge City in 1866.

What was the distrust all about? After a while, it became obvious to me that I was being distrusted simply because I posed questions, because I was somehow, through my questions, refusing to let life be lived. I was just too much like all the other planners and surveyors and social workers who were always coming around with questionnaires and interview forms. These people just didn't have anything formal to say to me, and yet here I was again with my questions. That was when I decided to try an entirely new tack. I devised a remote destination for myself and then would stop at a house to ask questions about getting there on foot. After obliging me as best he or she could, the householder sometimes grew curious about me. How did I get lost? Why did I want to walk all the way out there? Was I sure I knew where I was going? If the person was white, this would inevitably lead to a discussion of "human relations" in Compton. If he or she were black, it might go no further than an inquiry into where I was from: "New York, you say . . . a lot of people from the East out here. But not too many of them in Compton."

With many residents of Compton (black or white), I got the impression that being an Easterner almost immediately marked me off as a Jew, and that was, no doubt, a further basis for the distrust, but the core of it went much more deeply, was truly more fundamental, than their perfunctory, but almost obligatory, hostility to "exotics." It was compounded, in part, out of the distrust they felt for one another. No one I met ever referred me to an acquaintance as the sort of reliable person to whom I should speak about Compton. In part, it also had to do with their peculiarly die-hard sense of caste, their radical individualism. These people really did feel all alone, most of the time; and that is why it was so important that one come at them as if one were a "regular guy."

After a while, it became apparent that it was not me they distrusted; they distrusted just about everybody. There was the Vietnam war all over the newspapers, and they distrusted you if you spoke about it; yet they seemed to distrust you even more, when you attempted to pass over it, to be discreet. The same was true of Meredith's shooting. If you talked about it, you were probably a "nigger lover." But if you didn't, and yet told them you were from New York, you were probably just a more discreet version of a "nigger lover."

The headlines about black power, which were just beginning to come out of Mississippi, gave off a kind of terrifying echo in the suburbs of Watts, where many people thought they had already had a taste of what black power meant only the previous summer. They really hadn't liked what they had tasted, even those Compton Negroes who still tried lamely to defend black power; and, with Stokely

Carmichael and his colleagues speaking out against the war in Vietnam, many citizens of Compton, whether black or white, didn't like people tut-tutting their war effort, either.

Most of the conversations I had never reached very rarefied levels of discourse. Generally, we talked about the weather ("We never seem to have any Spring any more"), about what young people were doing ("they have no respect for anybody"), about the Berkeley students ("Some of them ought to be in Vietnam"), about the high cost of living ("The President is a rich man. I have to laugh when he tells my wife to tighten her belt"), about the War on Poverty ("Some of Johnson's friends are getting awful rich off that one . . . a lot of poor people too"), about Ronald Reagan ("He seems like he's got guts, and that's more than I can say for Pat Brown"), but mostly about what was happening to Compton. The town was being engulfed by Negroes (if one happened to be a white man), or sold down the river by the landlords in Beverly Hills (if one happened to be Negro), and the situation looked hopeless. The further I penetrated into the so-called good neighborhoods of town, the fiercer was this distrust syndrome, the more explicit the sense of hopelessness. Many people seemed to feel that they were only planning to stay in Compton "just a little while longer" because it was bound to get worse, and others felt betrayed that so many of their neighbors had already left. "Who do you think lives in Orange County now?" I was told by one of the town's leading merchants. "All my former customers."

There was, however, another cause for the feeling of distrust and betrayal which seemed to afflict so many Compton residents. It was their sense of having been abandoned in a most personal way by their own children, a feeling that after having made the sacrifices to find roots some place, those roots were withering, their plants being scattered to the winds. Nobody who still lived on in Compton seemed to have grown children living nearby. They were always at school some place, or working someplace else, or married and living someplace else, and the expectation was that they wouldn't ever be coming back, except, perhaps, on visits.

True, most of the people with whom I'd grown up no longer lived in Brooklyn, but, then again, neither did many of their parents, and wherever they did live—Long Island, say, or Westchester, or even Greenwich Village or the Upper West Side of New York City—it was really *like* Brooklyn. And they also seemed to carry Brooklyn with them when they went to college, or when they went overseas. But, from what I was told, Compton had always been regarded as just another way station. Most people seemed to recognize that their children were taking advantage of opportunities they'd never had themselves, but the parents still retained a certain feeling that they were acting haughtily, snobbishly, that the entire Compton experience was being obliterated, and this, I think, occasioned most of the vituperation about "the way those young people carry on in Newport and Balboa," or about "those damned kids taking LSD."

Oddly enough, one didn't have to be over fifty to feel

this way. All one had to be was relatively immobile, fixed by either work, lack of education, or economic disadvantages in Compton. This lack of tolerance was as characteristic of the "salt-of-the-earth" working classes as it was of the merchants and white-collar workers and their wives; as characteristic of the men in work clothes in the beer and snooker parlors along Compton Boulevard as of the Rotarians at their weekly luncheons; and what it all seemed to be about was a feeling of resentment and of powerlessness when confronting new kinds of standards and manners, the expertise and power represented by an entirely new class. As one small merchant put it: "When your kid graduates college and he earns more money than you do and, not only that, gets to spend it any way he likes, with no accounting to me or his mother, it's darn hard not to feel a little funny about what you've helped to create.

"I mean," this man—a registered Unruh Democrat—told me, "my kid and I are always fighting. He says I don't understand about Negroes, but, then, he doesn't live here any more. He says I ought to take his mother on a European vacation, but, you know, he gets to go over there through his firm. He tells me I work too hard but he never seems interested in my business . . . and he wouldn't like it if I asked him to support me.

"The trouble with most kids today," he continued, "is that they make you feel like such a failure. Well, I'm wondering how well they would have done if they had been born thirty years earlier . . . I'm wondering if they even wonder about such things."

It is a fact that life expectations have changed so radically since the war that many young people now find it difficult to understand how their parents ever arrived at such standards. If work is no longer an imperative in the old sense, why be so conservative? If copulation doesn't necessarily lead to illegitimacy, disfranchisement, and perhaps shame and impoverishment, why not have a good time? And if there aren't any penalties for "consorting" with Negroes, then why not have Negro friends? It was this feeling of desperation in the face of a new elite, with not necessarily higher moral standards, but certainly many more options, that seemed so terribly embittering to so many Compton residents. Oddly enough, it wasn't necessarily through their sexual prudery or their racist fears that this bitterness was most often expressed, but through their feelings about work and money. They really seemed to believe that people weren't working as hard as they should be working, that the young people didn't know what work was all about; and they distrusted this new phenomenon. Was I working, for example, by going around asking all my questions? Whenever I told people I was a professional writer, their guardedness toward me would intensify. That was all very nice, they seemed to be saying, but you're not going to tell us that's the way you earn a living. Hardly! And what kind of work was it when a man's son stayed in college until he was 27 years old and then got himself his first job for $12,500 a year. No. Something was terribly wrong. The race was no longer to the swiftest in quite the same ways as it had once been. "People are no longer mak-

ing an effort," I was told: "It just doesn't pay." And when
these white people spoke of Negroes, their highest praise
was always directed toward the "ones who made an effort."
"He's a hard-working man," they would say, although they
all seemed to recognize that it wasn't necessarily hard
work which had brought about their children's present
prosperity. Nowhere was this made clearer for me than in
my conversations with Mike, a second-generation Armenian who was the proprietor of a small local supermarket. Mike's son was studying for his Ph.D. in linguistics
at California, and Mike's wife was so proud of him that she
kept a picture of him in cap and gown over the cash
register, but Mike wondered why it was taking the boy so
long "to get out into the world." "He's been in school all
his life," Mike said. "He's never been any place else. It's
not that I care. It doesn't cost me anything. I'm a proud
father . . . just as proud as she is . . . only what's going to
happen to a boy like that? Where does he think he's
going?"

Much later, Mike and I discussed his problems about
manning the store. It seemed he could never get trustworthy help. If they were trustworthy, they found better
jobs. If they weren't, it wasn't even worth the effort. I
asked Mike if he had ever hired Negroes. "They don't want
to work hard," Mike said. "They seem to resent it. I take a
kid. I try to train him to be a storekeeper and he seems to
resent it. They say why should I work for you six days a
week when I can get a job in downtown LA for five?
Honestly," he said, "they make me feel disgusted with my-

self sometimes . . . and I've got nothing to be ashamed about. I started out with nothing."

. . .

I shall not describe here the burgeonings of this new elitist class within our so-called Great Society. This report is chiefly about the class it is fast leaving behind, and about that class which is destined to be its proletariat. Shall one call the latter the *lumpen* consumers? Or perhaps the happiness sub-elite? They are just as likely to consume the recent Masters-Johnson report on human sexual response as they are new cars and mass-produced gourmet foods; and sometimes it seems that even their interest in jazz or LSD, folk-rock, happenings, or McLuhan is but another form of evanescent consumption. For these are the technicians, not the experts, the programers but not the executives, the social service workers but not the top professionals; and they merge with secretaries, admass people, production assistants, floating upper-lower Bohemians who drift from job to job with always something else in mind that they would much prefer doing. It's the absence of vocation which, as much as anything else, accounts for their liberal- 'ism. When it comes to self-interest, they seem like thoroughgoing believers in their own personalities.

And this sub-elite is characterized chiefly, if one can say they have any real character as a class, by their vocational transvestitism: They are not bound to their work, or defined by their work, or limited through their work. They aren't even willing to observe any of the taboos which work has customarily imposed. They don't have to. They are in demand. True, work gives them caste, mobility, the incomes through which they consume, but neither solidarity nor community, nor—more important—identity. It isn't their life. That's what takes place on the office telephone, or after hours in Redondo. It is to such persons, presumably, that the admen think they are addressing themselves when they show us that lovely blonde elevator operator, dressed like Johnny in the Philip Morris ads, rushing off her job to try out the new Mustang. "She felt like a bird in a gilded cage," the voice of the announcer declares, "until one day..."

Unfortunately, most of us still can't walk right off the job and buy ourselves a Mustang whenever we feel blue, but we can visit the psychiatrist, take in a film, get high, and in California, take a swim, or a drive, go surfing, or— more likely— change our job. Consequently it is the increasing absence of the sense of caution, through which the older lower middle classes advanced themselves, that is the chief stylistic innovation of the lumpen consumers. In Compton one is likely to find grade-school teachers dressed like beatniks, and civil servants eating lunch in topless joints. Like those whom fortune has destined to be their intellectual betters (with all the rewards which that now entails), these people seemed to envisage lives that were so fluid, so mercurial, that they were as likely to be teaching grade school in Saudi Arabia next year as in South Gate this year. One pretty young woman put it this way: "This

year I'm working in Watts. Next year I just plan to lie in
the sun in Puerto Vallarta."

So it was as if all the children of the sturdy blue- and
white-collar classes were setting out to be Holden Caulfield,
Huck Finn, or, better yet, Felix Krull. Even Jay Gatsby's
dream had been swept to one side, and the *Playboy* ethic
was subverting the old privateering spirit into entirely novel
concepts of personal gain. Not very difficult to understand,
therefore, why so many of their elders distrusted them. For
better or worse, they *had* committed themselves; they were
entrenched, but threatened, terribly insecure in asserting
what they were. Not only had the older generation and this
radically mobile group "split," but they felt increasingly
fearful that they might necessarily have to retreat if these
others were to get their way. And retreat meant the style
of life represented by the streets surrounding Noni's Indian
Sycamore, which is why they were suspicious of the
neighborhood, why it had to be obliterated so that there
wouldn't be any reminders of it, no place left to fall back
upon. For these respectable Compton householders had
spent their entire lives being schooled about their limitations. They had their own children to thank for being instructed in their inadequacies. Meanwhile, they had years
to live out, and they were determined not to give up. The
forms they still endeavored to live out were more than just
soporifics against their bitterness. Their bigotries, their
narrow-mindedness, their gardening, if you will—these
were their ways of asserting their own class dignities against
the aimless depredations of a new class which had dispensed

with dignity, which asserted only its liberation, and which seemed to be carrying on a revolution of sorts with no more sublime Utopia in mind than that which is represented by the notion of "relating to one another."

No wonder that so many people in Compton still put out their flags on Memorial Day, and then write indignant letters to the local papers about their neighbors who don't. It is not comfortable to find oneself defending a predictable chauvinism and narrowness, but was this, after all, being any less bigoted than the nice young social worker from Palos Verdes who confessed to me that she doubted if her mother ever had had a proper orgasm? "I mean," she said, "how can I have any respect for her when I know that's what her life has been like? She and my father, living together all these years, and you know I think they only did it once or twice a month, like defrosting the refrigerator."

Moments later, she was telling me why she personally detested Governor Edmund (Pat) Brown: "He's so indecisive."

I asked, "Do you suppose he's ever had a proper orgasm?"

"Don't be stupid," she said. "I can't even think about him that way."

I couldn't help wondering what Noni might have made of all this—or, even, Baxter and Rina. If one took this girl at her word, it now seemed as if the whole damned reservoir of respectability was being allowed to turn brackish before they'd even had the chance to take one nice, cool, thirst-quenching drink.

And then I thought about my bigot friend in the bar.

Between batters, he had peered up from the cradle of his arms just as I was about to leave and said, "Don't get me wrong. I got niggers working with me. That's one thing. I don't need them in my back yard."

Here, inside this little oasis of respectable, privatized hate, this man could spew to the end of days about niggers, but if he ventured outside, if he went off to work, there was a different decorum to be observed in which *he* and *they* seemed to have much more in common than, for example, I seemed to have with him. "Niggers," he might say, "they're not like you and me," but I was struck by my own alienation from him, and by the general alienation from him of that sub-elite class to which I seemed closest. What had he and I in common beyond our white skins? And what, beyond the most sentimental liberalism, attached me to Noni and Rina? At that moment, it all seemed like one of those terribly bitter family quarrels to which transcendental outsiders such as myself were not only unwelcome but could hardly pretend to participate in. And yet, whenever one thinks of the Negro masses and their poverty and neglect, one hopes that they will aspire to the good, the beautiful, and the true—to the life that one puts forward as one's own— whereas the extent of their tragedy (and it is a tragedy which education is helping to aggravate) is that they have not even been permitted the option of being able to afford for themselves such bigotries as that man was able to luxuriate in.

CHAPTER IV

TENDING TO THE GARDEN

"Some of the people say
what was he doing . . . some of the people
think I was crazy
and some people said
I was going to do something."

Simon Rodia, builder of the Watts towers

ccording to the Oxford English
Dictionary at least three different types of trees can be
called a sycamore: (a) a variety of the Middle Eastern fig
with mulberry-shaped leaves; (b) a large ornamental maple
introduced into Great Britain from the Continent to serve
as a shade tree on country lanes; (c) the North American
plane or buttonwood tree of the species *platanus*. Unfortunately, no such sycamores were to be found in the vicinity
of Noni's Indian Sycamore, but, one morning, I woke to
the piercing sweet odor of magnolias in bloom. The
strength of their perfume was such that I quickly had a
headache. A great bough full of waxy white blossoms had

opened overnight, and already some swollen brown-splotched husks were lying on the sidewalks like discarded melon rinds. Noni's oldest son was taking a broom to them. "Momma says they bring ants," he explained.

A few days later, the jacarandas, which had been in flower for nearly a month, began to shower their blooms across the sidewalks. I felt truly Botticellian, walking through streets carpeted with lavender petals. One of the most vivid sights I can recall is of a Negro teen-ager dressed for his high-school prom in a white dinner jacket and black bow-tie. Under one arm he carried a lucite box in which one purple waxy orchid reposed against silvery ribbons and tissue papers, as if embalmed.

Noni didn't garden. She claimed not to have the time. But she kept a pot of fuchsias in the office, a gift, she explained, from one of the neighbors, and I would occasionally see her watering them. Sometimes Noni talked to her plant: "Looks to me like you not long for this world . . . *uh uh* . . ." She would pinch off one of the withered leaves and stuff it into the pockets of her apron. None of the children were allowed near these fuchsias. Blake explained: "It's not that she's stingy. She just likes to have some things for herself."

When the magnolia tree blossomed, Noni told me it reminded her of the South. "Only there," she explained, "they stay on the tree a while longer. In Compton they are here today and gone tomorrow. I guess it's all this sun."

By day, Compton burned at you smoggily, causing the eyes to water. By four in the afternoon, these wreaths of smog were burned away by the bright hot sun. In the evenings the air was damp, and it had a malarial chill. Built into one of the walls of my room was a gas heater, but, after the first few nights, I kept it turned off. Otherwise, I would wake up in the morning with my mouth like an adobe cave.

I went to bed around 11:30 one evening, and ten minutes later a couple registered for the room next door. I heard the clump of two pairs of shoes, the flushing of a toilet, and then all was quiet, and I started to doze off. Fifteen minutes later, I was awakened by Noni's voice: "Get your hands off that! You can do what you like in the rooms but you just got to leave the plants alone." The next morning she told me that a man had tried to break off a "great big shoot of bamboo" to take back into his room. "Whatever for?" I asked. Noni squinted at me incredulously. "Some people gets their joy that way," she smirked. "They just like to get a licking."

On another evening, walking home from Flores' Cafe after dinner, I was greeted on Noni's corner by a tall thin Negro boy in a blousy yellow satin shirt. He wore tight black pants, smelled of lavender water, and was twirling a rose between his fingers. "Wouldn't you like to take me home with you?" he asked.

In general, though, Compton street life was about as staid as that of the suburbs of Luxembourg; and that's when I developed such an intense interest in people's gardens.

Almost any California town along the coastal strip has it all over its eastern cousins because of the variety of things which are growing most seasons of the year, and Compton is no exception. It was as if that bright golden air contained a continual haze of pollen and a swarming of bees, as if even under the hard, parched crust of the soil, life was boiling over. Amid all the obvious blight of shacks, tracts, tiny foundries, burnt-out, soiled, abandoned cars, the empty pot-holed gutters and the dusty lines of railroad ties, something always seemed to be sprouting. There were palm trees with great green gritty blades turning a leprous brown which grew to an astonishing height, peeling off a fibrous bark that fell against the curbs. I also recognized two or three varieties of eucalyptus, pepper trees, acacia, pear, apple and quince, broad Corinthian acanthus leaves shimmering darkly, and the lustrous dark green of lemon, orange, and citron leaves.

Such exuberant growth wasn't limited to the better parts of town. If anything, the illusion was that it flourished most where it was least cultivated. About the Sycamore there were flowering roots and bushes. Beyond a shack purveying auto mufflers and seat covers were enormous tangles of glistening purple and pink vines with great swollen petals and golden pollen dripping from their calyxes. Among the scrap heaps of a metal pressing shop, sweet peas bloomed, along with wild snapdragons. A parking lot behind the Elks Club had been fissured in hundreds of places by the spread of desert succulents; and there was mustard (and even what appeared to be buttercups) springing up beside the concrete flood control channels that were once the course of the Los Angeles River.

True, it was hard to imagine that only fifty years ago they had harvested considerable quantities of sugar beets just a few blocks from my motel, but Compton was not yet all concrete. One whole section of the community was still unpaved, and the characteristic bulrushes which had once covered the area still prevailed to the west of town. The worst sense one got was that the building boom in Compton had been so slapdash, so sleazy, so hectic in its appetite for devouring large tracts of earth and covering them up with just about any structure, but there was still enough open space so that one also got a sense of vacancy, and that made it all bearable. The old streets of town were umbrellaed by shade trees. It was only in the newer tracts, along the principal business street, and among the strict boxlike shopping centers, that the tyranny of concrete was complete.

And, even then, there was a certain desultory air to the place that made it somewhat more livable. Whenever city officials told me about the various beautification programs that were being proposed for Compton, I felt that left to its own neglect, the place would only be tawdry, but with an order imposed, it would be truly oppressive. In Compton, the eye was dazzled by thirty-foot-long hot dog signs and twenty-foot-high donuts, by brilliant automobile pennants flapping in the breeze, and by the blight of stucco store fronts turning yellow and cracking. In an era of pop art,

Compton seemed in the *avant garde*. Every business street seemed like an open invitation to greed and an acknowledgment of the acquisitive passion, yet even that was preferable, I suspect, to what the planners were hoping to do to it: to turn it into a large residential park of well-planned, green, open spaces inhabited by toy people with toy passions.

The Watts uprising had uncovered the real passions of those who had been barred from consumption, and the result was those patches of scorched earth throughout south-central Los Angeles, but it still didn't seem possible that anything could be as ugly or hermetic here as in claustrophobic Harlem, if only because there was still so much vacancy, so much wasted space, and within that space there was so much continual surging forth of growth, scrubby in parts but luxuriant in others, a kind of insistent vegetable world. Why, there were even two or three small farms—really, extended kitchen gardens, worked by Orientals—still within Compton city limits; and, if most Compton householders didn't have very much luck with their blue grass, the crab grass and weeds were doing remarkably well; 3 per cent of the town's acreage was still vacant land. Yet I was always depressed to discover, as I walked about, that nobody else seemed very cognizant of that aspect of the world which lay strewn about him. I used to stop pedestrians, schoolchildren, and even adults, to inquire what this or that unfamiliar tree or flower was called; and I rarely got knowledgeable answers.

One day I visited a local Head Start project, in which a

number of neighborhood women had been recruited as teachers' aides. They seemed like alert, intelligent people, absorbed by their zeal to uplift their own children, and the children seemed to be having a marvelous time at what they were doing. But what exactly were they doing? Painting airplanes, steamships, crude city scenes! Drawing automobiles, sputniks, and, oddly enough, African masks! Along with all these symbolizations of our modern world of speed, an effort was being made to bolster the children against the anomies of color in a racist civilization (for, hung on walls along with the fetishes, were photos of the Reverend Dr. King, of James Meredith, and even of Malcolm X), but it struck me that in the process a new order of anomie was being created; it was an almost deliberate alienation from the world in which the children were actually living. On the lawns of that little school there were profusions of brilliant California poppies growing wild, but none of the children were being taught about flowers, and most didn't seem to know that the trees shading the place were called palms. For all such children seemed to know, they could have been surrounded by plastic or even papier-mâché stage props—so disoriented were they from any organic sense of the world by the insistent blast of mass culture to which they were, albeit necessarily, being exposed.

The building which housed the Head Start classrooms also doubled as a Teen Post and a Community Center. There was television, a juke box, a coke machine. There were books about civil rights and Negro history, books by and about the Reverend Dr. King, racially integrated first readers, and a copy of Sammy Davis Jr.'s *Yes I Can*, but there wasn't anything about animals, flowers, birds or fish, the sea, the clouds, the stars. For myself, the order of abstraction to which such children were being encouraged to submit in the interests of their own eventual uplift was oppressive. For all its relatedness to the life most immediate to it, such a school might have been tunneled underground, or built on stilts four thousand feet above the earth.

What made this all doubly depressing was, of course, the fact that so many people in Compton were either one generation removed from the South, or even more recent immigrants. Within the memory of some of the adults (and even of some of the children) was a rural life in which one necessarily contended with the landscape. Now, in their efforts to achieve liberation from that life, they were consciously being instructed in how to obliterate all connectedness, to become mere abstractions like the rest of us, creatures of pure function. Unlike city children, they were not encouraged to play games of their own invention, but to participate in organized activities. Kicking desultorily at objects on the street, or running a stick along some fence posts to hear the rattle were also not encouraged. These children were to be instructed in the mysteries of technopol civilization.

Meanwhile, on the shabby streets encircling them, the white pensioners gardened, and so did a few of their black neighbors, pretending to take some pride out of the growth of their rose bushes, and perhaps wondering aloud, a trifle fearfully, about the attitudes which some of their newer neighbors had toward such behavior.

One shouldn't exaggerate this seeming dislocation (especially because the schools, with their ruthless utilitarianism, do so little almost anywhere else to reverse the trend), and yet its existence surely must make the lives of the suburbanized California Negro poor (with their still only-tenuous claims to a future) even more exasperating. They never quite seem to be living in the landscape, and yet their circumstances are such that they are less able to transcend it. Living on hope, they are really rooted no place. Invisible themselves, they are surrounded by a bitterness of abstractions: Black power! Community Action! It wasn't so much that one felt oneself opposed to such slogans, but to the tyranny of inorganic terms which they seemed to impose. Nearby, some Negro radicals were actually agitating to change the name of the Compton-Watts-Willowbrook conglomerate to Freedom City, and I couldn't help imagining a storefront burgeoning forth on Compton Boulevard: THE FREEDOM CITY BAIL BOND SERVICE.

One factor of California life that actively encourages the tyranny of the abstract—that is, the dependence on political idealism alone—is the absence of local political organization in the corrupt big-city Eastern sense of the words. With every Compton citizen a disinterested, nonpartisan voter, bosses must also be demagogues, and every issue is fought, not on the basis of partisan self-interest, but in terms of the most flagrant appeals to ideology and prejudice. Thus, an important school bond issue in Compton was argued in terms of whether or not the school superintendent had been prudent in carpeting and redecorating his office; and every candidate—from Pat Brown through Ronald Reagan—must play the populist of ubiquitous appeal because the pretense is that selfish interest should not and therefore does not exist.

It is on this same level of high abstraction that the conflicts of race are currently being debated. The liberal righteously sneers at the ignorant populism which resulted in the successful referendum to defeat open housing legislation, and demands a higher morality, but he is equally self-righteous about the old-style political bossism of state senator Jesse Unruh, who still seems to use something resembling an ethnic quota system to deal out political favors. And if he is truly liberal, that man will resent any power structure, whether it be labor-liberal, or banking-conservative, even though these may represent just about the only tendency toward resisting a candidate like Ronald Reagan.

But when everything is reduced to the ephemeral stuff of idealism, then the true tyranny of the abstraction holds sway. When Simon Rodia concocted those fantastic shell-encrusted spirals which twist above Watts like transubstantiated dream visions, he was exercising a higher morality (in that he was an artist), but he was also very much a man of his class, rooted, as it were, and not so unique as one may think in investing a particular place in a particular time with a portion of his life energies; other, less talented immigrants were also lining their lawns with abalone shells, or constructing heart-shaped bird baths and barbecue pits.

But it is doubtful whether very many Californians, even in Compton, still have any illusions about their rootedness, and this increasing sense of mobility (which, for the Negro, may still be largely a chimera), plus the vicious goading of the mass media, is what has reinforced the tyranny of the abstract to such a degree that the putative begins to supplant the possible, and mere euphemisms about "human relations" are substitutes for experience.

"I just hope you're not against Saul Alinsky," an assistant minister—a white man—challenged me one day by way of a greeting in the garden of his Willowbrook vicarage, preparatory to an interview about his self-help program for the black ghetto. When I assured him that—to my knowledge —I wasn't, he demanded to know what I thought about Malcolm X. After I had again exonerated myself from the suspicion of being antimilitancy, the minister himself appeared, a black man. "If you're opposed to Saul Alinsky," he started in by declaring, "there isn't much we have to say to each other."

Here I was, hoping to inquire about the likes of Congressmen Hawkins and Clawson, about a local politician such as Mervyn Dymally or Cleveland Wallace, and we were ideologizing about Saul Alinsky in Chicago. Fine enough, I suppose, but I just didn't see the relevance of that kind of talk between us at the moment, and my discomfort was such that I tried to change the subject. Lining the borders of the vicarage garden was a rich, sweet-smelling herb which gave off a lemony scent. I asked what this was. "Don't you think," I was indignantly informed, "it's a little too late to be talking about things like that?" But what seems equally true is that many Negroes and whites seem alienated by factors other than those originating through color.

There was, for example, a wholly different attitude toward Compton as a community. It wasn't only that the Negro lower middle classes tended to look down on many of their white neighbors as definitely mediocre, failures of a sort who, if it were not for the impediments of color, they might never have been obliged to live among, but they sometimes tended to view many of the efforts these people made to improve their community as some kind of reassertion of white supremacy.

Equally as real was the tendency of the whites to regard any attempts by Negroes to participate in the affairs of the larger community as a form of "takeover." If a local Negro leader made anti-Vietnam remarks, it somehow seemed twice as insidious as when a white man did. But, in truth, just about everybody, black and white, seemed to be repressing the war in Vietnam; perhaps that is why the outbursts of the "militants" seemed so shrill.

"If ever America undergoes great revolutions," De Tocqueville wrote, "they will be brought about by the presence of the black race on the soil of the United States; that is to say, they will owe their origin, not to the equality but to the inequality of condition.

"When social conditions are equal," he continued, "every man is apt to live apart, centered in himself and forgetful of the public. If the rules of democratic nations were either to neglect to correct this fatal tendency or to encourage it from a notion that it weans men from political passions and thus wards off revolutions, they might eventually produce the evil they seek to avoid, and a time might come when the inordinate passions of a few men, aided by the unintelligent selfishness of the pusillanimity of the greater number, would ultimately compel society to pass through strange vicissitudes. In democratic communities revolutions are seldom desired except by a minority, but a minority may sometimes effect them."*

In Compton, one saw revolution and counterrevolution taking place within the same continuum. Around Medgar Evers Square, the householders sat behind closed doors, waiting to hear the welcome thud every Thursday afternoon of their subscription copies of *Muhammad Speaks* against their doorsteps; and the white Birchites chased the schoolchildren from their streets, or sat alone in their bars cursing their bad luck to have been left behind. But the majority of Compton residents were "persons of good will." It was not "unintelligent selfishness," nor even "pusillanimity" which retarded their efforts to create a community. It was opportunity, mobility, the future. "I've got my kids to worry about," everybody kept saying. Or, as one Compton householder put it: "I expect my kids to get everything they can out of this place and then move on to greener pastures. There are just too many opportunities in the world to settle for a place like this."

* *Democracy in America*, Vol. II, pp. 270–71, Doubleday Anchor edition.

Unfortunately, for far too many Compton kids, the "greener pastures" to which they were moving on were in South Vietnam. Yet it was even possible to see beyond that immediate future. Driving to LA one day, I picked up a young hitchhiker. He had returned on furlough from Vietnam only the week before. I asked what it had been like. "Awful," he said. "The VC may not be winning the war, but they don't have to. At this point, most of us would just like to give them the place and say to hell with it." I asked if most of his buddies felt that way. "It's like everything else," the kid said. "They come over thinking they're going to do a job, and then they get pretty cynical."

A moment later, he was adding: "They say the Russians make propaganda. What does our government do? My folks don't even know what it's like. They don't know how many of our boys are getting killed over there. The government never tells them that . . . and we don't know why we're fighting."

Just before I dropped him off at the Civic Center, this veteran of perhaps nineteen said, "Don't get me wrong. I'll be glad to go back there. It makes you mad to listen to what people here are saying. I've got a lot of buddies over there, and they're good guys. But if you were to watch television, you would think we were all just like the Nazis. I don't get it. They send us out there and then they tell us to behave like gentlemen."

It struck me that here was one of the few people of Compton I'd met who still took pride in his work. But what kind of work was he doing? And what if the war dragged on through another half a decade of the same bloodletting?

It was the kind of bitterness one heard in Paris in the 1950's from those who chanted "*Algérie Française.*"

CHAPTER V

TOPLESS!

———————————————

Something had definitely gone all wrong in Compton. It was as if the whole town had a belly-ache from too much ice cream. Everybody was cross with everybody else. A whole town turned sour. Everybody feeling as if they'd been "had."

As soon as I got there, the torpor set in. If you've ever been had—had so that it really makes your ears burn—you feel like you would simply like to hide somewhere. Any place. I felt that way, and so I began to stay rather close to Noni's which didn't help me very much. At the Sycamore, people were having one another regularly, and they called it, at best, lovemaking. Later, there were the usual recriminations:

"I'm glad for you. I really am."

"So next time, maybe we'll try it my way?"

"Every time we try it like that my leg just goes to sleep on me. I'm all pins and needles right now."

Human beings do a poor job of making love to one another. They flail about ineffectually, and are always busy conceptualizing. The "erect swaggering waddle" prior to coitus, which Bingham observed in the male chimpanzee and called the "sex dance," has no relationship whatsoever to the manner in which Noni's guests would meander up to her registration desk to inquire about rooms. In fact, I sometimes wondered if these all-too-ephemeral visitors were ever motivated by anything other than a perverse wilfulness, a desire to have done with it so that each could be alone with his miserable self again. The same old monotony forever rebeginning. Strip away all the hoary beards and superstitions, the taboos, the snide little secrets, and what have you? A pair of rather inefficient engines at work upon each other. No wonder it makes the schoolboys snicker. In Compton, the teen-agers swayed like cattails to a cynical new pop group called the Loving Spoonful, while their white elders wrinkled their brows over Negroes.

For there was, of course, the race question—but which race question?—and what did it have to do with such things as mass transit, pollution, higher taxes, or how to spend your leisure time? Who killed Kennedy? Are you for or against smog or police brutality? When there is dishonesty in high places and crime on the streets, where do you find decent sales help? Then there was the reading problem, and the population explosion, and the rise in water rates, and what to do about all those mothers on welfare, and why so many divorces, and the high cost of living. It was the kids, if you were an adult. It was adults, if you were a kid. Worst of all, things were so much better than ever. This was going to be the Great Society. But just how long would that last? And what would happen to all of us then? In the end, it was all the frayed ends of things, those numerous gaudy distractions, which drove everybody, including myself, to back away from thinking about mass murder. At the tip of our fingers was that self-inflicted wound called Vietnam. We'd stuck it just where it shouldn't have been. We said we didn't want to, but we did it anyway, and now it was infected, but not so sore that we were willing to go to the doctor for radical surgery. It hurts them as much as it hurts us. They're just bound to give up sooner or later.

"My son is with the First Cav at Iadrang," a man down the block from Noni's greeted me one day, proudly, from his garden fence.

About all I could say was, "Wonderful!"

"Do you know what the boys drink in the First Cav?"

I didn't have the foggiest idea, and I said so.

The man announced, "Would you believe beer and tomato juice?"

"Beer and tomato juice?"

"I'm not kidding," he said. "I saw it on the TV."

Television, according to some moralists, is a form of escape, but in Compton one escaped through TV to LBJ, Bobby Kennedy, Mark Lane, and beer and tomato juice. Occasionally, there were also U.S. soldiers burning down Vietnamese villages, but whoever bargained for that? It was as if we'd gone to bed with a pain in the finger, and awakened with a sty.

And then everybody turned cynical and sour, or else they went topless.

I use topless here, in its most general sense, to mean no dignity! No risks! No class! For that's about what it amounts to. The old lower-middle classes pulling off their shirts and saying, "Why not? Everybody else is getting away with it, so why the hell not? I don't have to worry about my neighbors. Look! They're all sitting there in the audience!"

When radicals used to believe that the shirtless classes could some day seize power through a redemptionist act of the corporate will, rhetoric still held the masses of men in its sway, and there was one set of rules for public life and another for private life. But what happens when all the old public petit-bourgeois high seriousness vanishes, and suddenly exists only in the mind? When your enemies are you, not *they*? When your public morality and your private parts are supposed to mesh? When the spread of affluence is so incredible that the shirtless classes begin to merge with the topless classes?

Ah then, a specter will still linger to haunt us, but it will be that of a naked woman with a light bulb in her belly button: The Tropical Fish! The Topless A Go Go! The Titillator! Or perhaps the Box! No matter which way one drove through Compton, eventually he had to run into such places: The Gam Room! The Sacred Triangle! The Nut

Club! It was as if, having banished forever certain kinds of lower-middle class caution and shame, the residents of that part of the "Southland" were now intent upon making everybody around them aware of their marvelous candor.

"Would you believe TOPLESS?" a faded sign, somewhere near Pepperdine on the road to Watts, perorated. Imagine, too, nakedness as pluralism: every race, class, caste, and ethnic order represented, a mulligan stew of naked breasts, buttocks, and legs and arms dispensing food and drinks. Near Gardena, where the topless girls were all Oriental, one place advertised chow mein family dinners. Toward Watts, topless took on a shabby negritude; I saw one place decorated with spears and African masks. A number of shabby Mexican joints were spattered through East Los Angeles. Of the Caucasians who'd started the ball rolling to begin with, one saw them topless just about every place else: decked out for the visiting firemen along Sunset Strip, or topless with freckles in Long Beach, Hollywood, San Bernardino. Once, caught in a taffy pull of downtown freeways, I wandered by mistake into a topless drive-in and was served a rare hamburger and a chocolate frosted at my window by a pretty young blonde in short shorts, white boots, and a transparent plastic halter.

In Compton, one of the customers told me, "I'm just finding it harder and harder to bear down like I used to . . .

"Oh, I know what you're thinking," he added, "a man like me with a wife and a kid in college and responsibilities. Well, that's just it. I don't begrudge anybody anything, but even my doctor says I should take it a little easier." When I asked him what he did, he snapped: "Vending machines . . .

"Between here and Boyle Heights, I got 150 machines," the man said, "and I tell you sometimes it just gets to be too much for me. I mean, I have to see each one personally a couple of times a week, just like you would with a real person because sometimes they break down, and even if I could get it, I can't afford any help. You want to know why? Sure I'll tell you. What the customers don't steal they would . . .

"So when it's getting to be like this I just come here and sit awhile and have a drink and watch the show and maybe I talk to the girls and maybe I don't. Why not? It's all perfectly innocent."

And perhaps it was except that when one went off to the men's room, there were all those self-advertisements scribbled on the stalls:

Ring and valve jobs done . . . while you wait!
Need your tubes flushed? Call Amy.
CARTE BLANCHE—DINER'S CLUB—OR CASH—
CALL PATRICIA—READY CASH

And sometimes there were more elusive things scratched into the tables:

If you like fresh fish, try Venice.
COME to the Century Plaza Hotel.

Or even:

Help! I'm a nymphomaniac.

And there would be a telephone number.

Occasionally, too, there would be political notes:

MAO TSE-TUNG SUCKS

Or:

*Mother fuckers! Big white pricks!
Here's to Watts 66!*

Or even:

Ronald Reagan has a cute ass.

And once:

From Santa Barbara to the Saltan Sea, guess who is taking over?

And everybody looked and giggled and said it wasn't anything, nothing very much there at all, just as they stared at the wiggling fannies and wobbling breasts and that too wasn't anything. Hardly worth looking at! Just there! Another part of the landscape. Perfectly innocent.

Which it was, I suspect, because none of the working men who entered and left such places at lunch time, coffee break, or dinner seemed as if they were staggering through an erotic stupor. Nor did I find any evidence that this prickly heat of topless bars, supper clubs, snooker joints, and beaneries was having even the slightest effect on production quotas at the nearby North American plant. In Compton's divorce court—which I attended for many hours at a stretch—men and women haggled over support payments and tiny scraps of community property, but no-

101

body ever called the other a bitch or a greedy frigid two-timer. But the clients were very nearly topless. Some just wore slacks and T shirts. Or the women wore sun dresses and even pedal pushers. With all of Compton in various stages of deshabille, why not go the whole hog?

For myself, I always found it rather disconcerting to have a woman lean over to serve me beer, topless. Yet I came to appreciate the charm of the thing. If this was supposed to be a lower-middle-class Garden of Eden before the Fall, there had to be places where you could simulate original nature. It was also as if the entire state of California had been set aside for the frivolous, to be governed, perhaps, by a different set of rules than the rest of the country, or at very least, by those rules laid down solely by climate. It was just a trifle Levantinized, as they say in Israel, and that is not to refer to the "race question." It was in the way people looked—black or white, middle class or poor. Once, in a topless joint near Venice, I came across a grandmotherly woman knitting a sweater. "It's for my boy in Vietnam," she explained. "I don't know whether he needs it or not, but I just think maybe he ought to have one over there."

Others have commented on the dry jewel-like opulence of Southern California, the way an entire landscape seems to be bragging about its liberation from necessity of any kind, even though some people here are working just as hard, if not harder, than elsewhere, but when you "make it" under such circumstances—I mean really "make it"—what do you do? Once, driving south near the Long Beach freeway, I passed a billboard which was decorated in the form of a greeting card. A prominent local businessman had purchased the space to send felicitations to his wife on their wedding anniversary. Clearly, it wasn't simply that he had prospered and wanted the whole vehicular world between Los Angeles and San Diego to know about his good fortune, which he attributed, in part, to a faithful mate. Nor was this simply a self-advertisement that would inevitably redound to his credit, be good for business. Perhaps the man had sounded himself, found his feelings genuine, and then decided that, after all, happy marriages in California are few and far between and why not bang the drums a little, make a little publicity. Besides, the wife—or perhaps one of her friends—driving by would just have to see the way he felt. You couldn't miss it. So, likewise, as one girl put it, "if you've got nice breasts, why hide them?"

Yet many of the girls were quite homely. Still others had been so depilated and cosmeticized that they no longer resembled flesh and blood at all, but were like plastic mannikins—abstractions again! And sometimes there were just as many women as men customers in the place. Was this simply more of the same cynicism and abstraction? When one gets cynical about sex and nudity, there is not much left. Perhaps we shall all go shopping topless some day on mildly heated sidewalks that move so that the breasts wobble a little, but not so much that they make an unpleasing picture. Then, shall we also go to work topless? Obviously, some Californians already are.

One needs only to enter any of the supermarket drug stores serving the residents of Watts or Willowbrook to have the point driven home with a vengeance. Along with all the old so-called necessities of family life, one finds marked-down martini shakers, picnic baskets, tiny alice bathing briefs for men, topless suits, "No-Doze" pills, and fruit-flavored wines (as if grape-flavored wine were distasteful), and it is difficult to browse through such stores with a set of shopping priorities in mind. Perhaps that explains why so many of them were burned and looted in August of 1965. Although a variety of sophisticated psychosocial mechanisms have been cooked up to describe the resentments of the poor which, ultimately, might have exploded in looting, it seems reasonable to suppose that once law and order broke down in Watts, all the old artificial distinctions about private property also broke down. The looters didn't feel barred from having *things* by their poverty or their enforced "leisure." Indeed, living in opulent California, topless now just like everyone else, was it wrong for them to suppose that they had been encouraged to feel a little less than cautious?

The latest and most vicious trend in the long process which denudes you even as it enriches is the no-minimum-balance regular unlimited checking account. Whenever I drove up toward central LA through the residential streets, I was exhorted on the car radio by jingles and homiletics that Security First National (or, perhaps, some other set of abstractions meant to imply a "financial institution") was willing to write me all the checks I cared to write, no balance necessary, if I would call a certain number at once, and none of them would ever bounce. A whole nation "hanging" checks on one another! If I lived in Watts or Compton, it would certainly sound a lot better to me than Welfare, or even, even twenty dollars a week plus welfare in a "work-orientation program" of the War on Poverty.

CHAPTER VI

KARL MARX OR
FREDERICK DOUGLASS?

Whole town behaving just like niggers," Mike, the Armenian grocer, declared, "and all the niggers here are very respectable."

There was some truth in what he was trying to get at. In Compton the fiercest upholders of the old rectitudes were likely to be black. Or so it sometimes seemed.

For it was representatives of black Compton who regularly appeared in sizable numbers at City Hall meetings approximately every fortnight, although, of course, in the spirit of former Governor Hiram Johnson, the meetings were open to all. But the whites never came. They were always somewhere else, and if a few did attend, they did not demonstrate that they had much to talk about. They just made sounds, or cracked cynical jokes. At first, about the only whites I ever saw in attendance were the sales managers of firms which had complaints to make against the City Manager for not awarding them contracts in one or another sealed bidding.*

Likewise, it was black Compton which pushed hardest for a local antipoverty program and then worried hardest about prorating the bill equitably so that Lynwood, Paramount, etc., were made to pay their shares. Of course, they had allies, strong supporters among the social welfare professionals, the white liberals, the "civic-minded," but, in the main, the demands of these allies sounded increasingly shrill and abstract, while, to the Negro community, simple fairness was still something to be craved.

No wonder that Negroes in Compton had a reputation for being "pushy." The Mexicans said so, and the whites sometimes said much worse. But if you became cynical about the value of an education, you had only to talk with the housewives of black Compton. If you turned sour on getting ahead, the most impassioned defenders of the old ethic turned out to be black. For such people, the idea of self-government still had an aura which a lot of other people had poured down the drain long ago. These black families were still only a small elite, hardly all of black Compton, just the activists, and fundamentally conservative about who governed whom about what, but weren't there any white activists left in town? Didn't they have any demands to make for fairness and equity? Or was it all grumbling in the bars about "niggers"? The great tragedy of the Negroes

* One reason may largely be that the Negroes had their one big issue—equality—whereas the whites had both all issues and no issues. They were just part of what we call current events.

107

seemed to be that, increasingly, they had hardly anybody to integrate with but an elevated "poor white trash."

Not that there weren't power elites and service clubs and bridge parties where people talked politics, but the public rhetoric at such gatherings was always either self-congratulatory or xenophobic; and somewhere toward the middle of the evening, one would usually be accosted by a retiring-looking fellow who would say: "This is all just a lot of non-sense, what they're talking about. I never take any of this seriously."

More cynicism? But where was it all leading? In the main, it was leading white people right out of Compton. It also meant that the sense of "community," which Office of Economic Opportunity functionaries were hoping to encourage across America, had about as much chance of living up to their mysterious guidelines about maximum feasible participation (or even of taking hold in Compton at all) as the rituals of the Swedenborgians. What community, and just who would be living within it? What would it all be about? If the whites ever seemed worried about things like day-care centers and new libraries, they never seemed to show it. And one thing was certainly clear: you weren't going to get black Compton (that is, its elites) to strut around topless. They still thought they had a claim to stake out for the dignity of man. Having staked those claims chiefly through the rhetoric of the Constitution, they were still convinced believers in the Social Contract; they believed that a man's a man, and in all the rest of the Enlightenment baggage, and some still even had grit.

Most Americans worry terribly about past, present, and especially the future, and what it will "have in store" for us. As a consequence, we are basically conservative. In Compton, nearly everyone was too, but their conservatisms differed. Some were acquisitive about pleasure; others still hungered for worldly goods. Sometimes they were merely ignorant and xenophobic. Most often, such conservatism was a way of saying: "What do you expect of me? What do you want from my life?" Or perhaps: "You ought to be ashamed of yourself to make such demands."

Then there was the conservatism of those who just wanted to set everything aright. They seemed to believe that, once, things had been a good deal better. Things had to have been a good deal better, and if only they could be set right again, if only people once again respected other people's rights, if only merit were recognized and good conduct rewarded, then it might make sense to try to do one's level best to keep things in order. But, in the meantime, in between times, why not, as they say, go just a little topless? And for some odd reason, the Negroes, those who suffered most under the old conservatism, also seemed to find a great deal of merit in this argument.

.　.　.

The National Council of Negro Women was holding an art exhibit in the Compton City Hall. My guide, a local housewife with a henna-red wig, showed me the clumsy still-lifes of fruits and vegetables, the rather too-orange

Cezanne-like landscapes, the Rivera-like drawings of Mexican peons, and then stopped in front of a black-and-white oil portrait of a man with a thick shock of beard, a high forehead, deep-set eyes, a string bow-tie. His costume was Lincolnesque, the jowls heavy and Europeanized, and the glazed white face had a pasty look about it that was further accentuated by a sober costume consisting of a waistcoat and jacket. He seemed to be gnawing earnestly on a portion of his lower lip.

I thought I recognized the man. "Who's that?" I asked. "Karl Marx?"

She gave me a look of extreme annoyance. "Certainly not. That's one of our great heroes, Frederick Douglass. Haven't you heard of Frederick Douglass?"

Was it my fault that this portrait was so bleached out that I had assumed the mulatto face to be that of a white man? I said, "Don't get me wrong. He just looked very much like Marx . . . or perhaps Brahms," I added.

"It's a shame what they don't teach you white boys about our history," the woman said.

I said, "I didn't mean it as an insult. Marx and he . . . they just happened to look alike. After all, they lived through the same era. In fact," I added, "Marx wrote some very fine stuff for the New York *Tribune* during the Civil War."

"Well, this isn't Marx. It's Frederick Douglass," and the woman marched angrily away from me. I began to understand why. A group of Compton civil servants had gathered in the corridor to listen to our dialogue. I had committed an unpardonable sin by saying the name of Karl Marx in public. Probably my hostess would be judged by the company she kept. She was standing as far away from me as possible, pretending to study a cubist still-life of abalone shells and calabashes. By myself now, I searched the features of the former slave, as if to inquire if he also would have felt ashamed for being confused with Herr Marx of the New York *Tribune*. Then the woman said, "Come to think of it, he does look a little like one of the Smith Brothers."

Throughout my stay in Compton, I was usually surprised and depressed by the flagrant political and social conservatism of the people I met. It seemed to lack any historic sense. It was just a groping about for the familiar and reassuring. As reported earlier, on the day I arrived in Compton, the social workers of the County Bureau of Public Aid (Welfare) went out on strike. As I drove down West Compton Boulevard, I saw their line of attractive, well-dressed, mostly Negro men and women carrying placards and assumed, automatically, that it was a civil rights demonstration. Eventually, I was able to park my car and went over to chat with some of the pickets.

None of them wanted to talk with me. When they paraded past where I stood, they would raise their signs demanding higher wages and fewer case loads, and one older woman even gave me a leaflet, but when I stopped her on her next time around to ask some questions, she said, "I'm just a worker. You'll have to speak to one of our leaders."

Indeed, so pervasive was their suspicion of someone

111

actually taking an interest in their grievances that the result was almost the same when I was finally approached by one of the leadership. "If you're from the press," the young man said, "you'll have to talk to somebody from our strike committee."

"I'm not from the press," I explained. "I'm a writer who just happened to be in town, and I was wondering what the strike was all about and if you're getting much support from your clients."

"You'll have to talk to our strike committee," the young man said, through tight lips, as he walked away.

Later in the day, I happened to walk past the picket line again, and the same young man said: "Hi!" We shook hands, and I asked how the strike was going. He was obviously depressed about the prospects of a favorable settlement. It was turning out that the County just wasn't very concerned about not having its social workers visit its clients, although the young man claimed they would be concerned when it came time to apply for their state and federal reimbursements. A group of the other workers presently gathered around us. I asked if any of them lived among their clients in Compton. None did. In fact, they seemed rather offended (and somewhat defensive) about my comments about their not living where they worked. "You wouldn't understand," one young man said. "It's not a matter of prejudice. It's just not the kind of place where I would like to live."

"It's very dead here," a pretty blonde girl put in.

"Maybe if I had a family, I would feel differently," a well-dressed Negro youth added, "only I don't have a family . . . and I really don't know if I would live here even if I did."

Our conversation had reached an embarrassing impasse. I was anxious to move on, but didn't want to seem rude now that I had, at last, struck up an acquaintanceship. I asked, "Is it tough getting Welfare in California? I mean, what would I have to do if I wanted to apply?"

"You apply?" They were all very amused. One girl said: "I really don't think you could apply." Someone else asked, "Say, where are you from, and what are you doing here?"

When I explained how I had come to write a book about life in Compton, they immediately froze up solid once again. Then the leader said: "Come on, everybody, let's get back on that line."

As they walked away from me, I heard an older woman say, "I don't know about you, but I don't like being pumped!"

Later, in a nearby luncheonette, I ran into some of the workers a third time. They were sitting around over ice-cream sodas, gossipping. I went to the counter and ordered a sandwich. Then I overheard one of the girls talking to a co-worker: "He wanted to know if we had a strike fund or would we have to go on Welfare. Now what kind of question is that?"

The conservatism of nearly everybody I met in Compton was, of course, of a limited variety. It did not, as already indicated, necessarily dictate a style of life in which one saved one's money, worked earnestly at a job, was prudent about consumption. Many people seemed to resent the kind of quasi-fundamentalist conservatism represented by those who are behind Ronald Reagan. They were, however, equally as resentful of the corrupt "one-hand-washing-the-other" egalitarianism of the Pat Brown Democrats. There was a point of indignation about values and social classes which they found it difficult to suppress. They wanted to look up to their betters and were being constantly disappointed. They wanted to believe in the beatitude of the poor, the weak, the humble, and they were always being disillusioned. Most were newcomers to California who managed in a short time to regard other newcomers like myself as outsiders and intruders. One learned this quickly on the various "talk-back" programs over radio, in which the subject of race was an occasion for the most blatant kinds of chauvinism. "I don't understand. If they're coming here to live," one woman with an Iowan twang might say of the people of Watts, "why they can't behave like Californians."

Or: "The colored people are getting things we never got . . . and we didn't dare to do some of the things they do!"

Or: "It's not my fault they're Negroes. What do they want from my life?"

With the older people, there was an anger to their voices and to the way they referred to their lives that was not so easy to pass off as mere bigotry. But with the very young, the process was at once more frightening and disturbing. The unruly white youths who were hauled into Municipal Court nearly every day for drunk driving, driving without a license, brawling—what was one to make of such youngsters? Against whom was their grievance? Why were even their most perfunctory glances around the courtroom like insults? And what was one to make of those who had mastered their lives sufficiently to gain a measure of education and mobility and still seemed dead-set in the middle of nowhere? None seemed to have homes. They were the transients who lived together in little privatized colonies of fun-seekers near Newport and Balboa, and never even admitted that they saw their parents. Yet about matters of class morality, they could still be very conservative. The poor *should* work. They *should* be taught to save their money and not have too many children. They *should* want to send their children to college. It was as if, in an entirely humorless way, these newly forged representatives of the California educational system were entirely unconscious of the fact that at least some of the poor might have viewed such personal progress and liberation as a detriment—that, in fact, they did not want their children exposed to such influences for fear that they would then no longer even have their children.

It is, admittedly, difficult to ignore this kind of poor man's conservatism; one must take note of it. During my summer in Compton there was much talk by the educated liberals of the town about the Moynihan Report on the breakdown of the urban Negro family, and it seemed to come up in nearly every conversation in Compton as the ultimate judgment on the Negro poor. But it was striking to me that it came from those who had successfully cast off their own family ties and were now part of a floating classless sub-elite. I remember one young homosexual advertising copywriter telling me that family life was "a crucial thing." I don't think he was being a hypocrite, but he was caught up in a general bewilderment; for, moments after he told me this, his boyfriend regaled me with a story of how they had gone to look for a place to live the previous week-end and had ended up buying a brand-new house.

"If I make it cheaper for you to buy than to rent," their salesman had told them, "would you perhaps consider buying?"

And when they hesitated just a little, he quickly added: "Come on now. You don't want to live in a second-hand house. *Nobody* wants to live in a second-hand house."

CHAPTER VII

EPITAPH ON AN ARMY OF
MERCENARIES

I f one wants to learn about what's been happening in a small town, a good place to begin is in the morgue of the local newspaper, but when I asked permission to glance through some of the bound back issues of Compton's leading newspaper, they said it couldn't be done. "He doesn't like strangers back there," I was told.

"But," I protested, showing my press credentials, "I just wanted to see what Compton was like ten or fifteen years ago."

"I don't care if you're from *The New York Times*," a busy editor parried, "if *he* wouldn't like it, then it can't be done." Presently I was being shooed out of his office.

He was the Colonel, publisher of the paper, a former Compton mayor, and said to be one of the most powerful men in southern California. During my first official visit to Compton, I had listened almost every day to remarks about the personal likes and dislikes of this man, but we had never met. Most of the time, he was simply referred to as *he* or Colonel. When I came back to Compton the second time, this is what I was told:

It was said that *he*—being a Georgia-born Democrat—didn't "particularly like minority groups."

It was said that he had once been an enthusiastic New Dealer until the unions had tried to organize his business.

It was mouthed about that if you wanted to be a Judge, an assistant DA, or even a tax assessor, you had better be on the right side of the Colonel.

It was even rumored that one important local politician, who managed to get on the Colonel's wrong side, regularly used to find his picture cropped from all the ceremonial photos that were taken for the various local editions of the Colonel's papers.

Not a very pretty picture to print of Compton's leading citizen, but most of the time there were no insults intended. If anything, some of these comments often were made admiringly; the Colonel managed to play the game by his own rules, and many Compton residents seemed only too willing to grant him this privilege. He was, after all, a self-made man who had gained his present high esteem through the force of his own personality. Starting with a couple of supermarkets, the Colonel had built up a chain of sleazy "shoppers" into the third- or fourth-largest newspaper empire in the county; and no one yet could say that he was getting too big for his own boots. The Colonel still paid his taxes in Compton; he still sent his children to Compton public schools; and, during most of the year he still lived in Compton, in a handsome, commodious but not terribly ostentatious ranch-style house on a modest street. And what if it was probably true—as some alleged—that the Colonel's power was such that he had forced even the telephone company to make a detour around his property with their poles and high-tension cables so as not to efface his view? The Colonel also did a lot of good for Compton, people said, a lot more than some of the grumblers. He was its chief booster. As one local businessman put it: "If you ask me, anybody who doesn't like what the Colonel stands for is either a sorehead or a Communist." But when I asked him what he thought the Colonel stood for, he added: "He doesn't stand for anything. He's just a regular guy."

"A regular guy" the Colonel was definitely not, but Compton seemed prepared to grant him the right to his dubious views because he, in turn, always feigned to extend a certain *noblesse oblige* toward those who managed to live up to his high standards of individual excellence. One Negro public office-holder told me:

"Clawson* is a bigot. The Colonel? He's just hard-nosed." And a prominent Negro matron who had socialized with the Colonel at a recent city function added: "He may not like my people, but he's willing to live with them on

* Representative Del(wood) Clawson, Republican, is congressman for the 23rd Congressional District, of which Compton is a part, and a former mayor of that city.

his terms. I know what you're thinking. How can I talk that way about a man who still thinks my husband is Stepin Fetchit, and that all Mexicans like to do is take *siestas* . . . Well, at least that man has got some spirit. Having him around, you know where the opposition is. It wouldn't be the same without him. I mean, once he said to me: 'I hear you're quite a hell-raiser.' I told him: 'Funny. That's what I heard about you too!' You know something? The Colonel seemed to think that *was* funny."

Wherever I went in Compton, there was evidence of the Colonel's influence and popularity. At meetings of the city council, political cynics would point out which councilmen were owned by the Colonel and which were not. Others would explain that the Colonel's power was really negligible nowadays in Compton "because of the Negroes," but that he still had tremendous influence "in Sacramento." And there always seemed to be a momentary lull before every vote of every council session as the office-holders pondered the political implications of their actions (i.e., what the Colonel might want them to do), although this did not necessarily mean that, as a mere publisher, he had every councilman's vote in his pocket. The chances were that he had none of them. His power over them derived, in part, from his unpredictability. The Colonel was a creature of such strong opinion and paradox that no one could have guessed what he thought about a given issue unless they were to consult with him directly, and, nowadays, he was out of town a great deal on long trips.

But, whether touring the globe with his grandson or

giving out awards to industrious newsboys, the Colonel's influence—his presence—in Compton was continually felt through the personality of his newspaper. He was just not the sort of man who hid his prejudices under a bushel. The rest of white Compton might be playing Tartuffe about the question of "human relations," but the Colonel came right out and said what he thought about trouble-making Negroes, and what he invariably seemed to be saying, on the basis of even one sample column, was that they were the chief cause of the increase in crime on the streets, that Martin Luther King was a dangerous agitator who was leading us all by the nose into civil mayhem, that Orientals couldn't be trusted, and neither could Frenchmen like De Gaulle, that the U.S. could end the war in Vietnam tomorrow if only it would "take" Hanoi and Haiphong. The Colonel's list of hates was constantly being refurbished through new additions, the stuff of his twice-weekly news-paper columns, which ran on the front page below a photo-graph of him.

These columns were little masterpieces of prolixity. He seemed to believe, for example, that the current agitation against the war in Vietnam was all the result of a weakening in American moral fiber, resulting from the influence of progressive education on the California school system. All of this, including his views on race, was done in a by-lined column, without the least deference toward the sensibilities of his growing Negro audience.

Yes, Negroes did buy the Colonel's paper. If they were searching for a home anywhere in the area, they had to, although one finds it difficult to account for the readership of those who were not.

One of the reasons why I chose to read through the Colonel's newspaper morgue was to check out a rumor which had been passed on to me by more than one Compton resident: that, during the statewide referendum against open housing, the Colonel's West Compton edition had supported open housing while his Compton edition had urged the electorate to vote for the referendum. Frankly, I doubted that the Colonel would find it necessary to take such a measure. He got most of the real-estate advertising in town no matter what he said. Once, the Colonel had even used his front-page column to excoriate a Philippine houseboy for arrogance because he had refused to work on a holiday. And when the column didn't suffice to get his point across, the Colonel might also commandeer an entire front page to write a by-lined editorial against a new school bond issue, for example, or to polemicize about the quality of the drapes in the school superintendent's office. Well, I wondered, if a man was willing to go that far on behalf of his convictions, why would he also want to be a hypocrite?

But, whether he wanted to or not, the Colonel's writings had a hortatory effect. They promoted a kind of double standard through which Compton's Negro population was barred from his society pages and always featured in the crime stories on his front pages. In Compton, any white person who wasn't in jail or on Welfare could make the society pages, so the absence of Negroes was noteworthy, and the stress on their various antisocial acts was more than just noteworthy; it was obsessive. But, again, there didn't necessarily seem to be any malice involved. Living in the midst of what he took to be an iniquitous sty, a Gehenna of vast and growing dimensions, the Colonel simply wanted his readers to face the same "facts" he was facing. Thus, glancing through his paper week after week, it was easy to believe that Compton was being preyed upon by roving hordes of barbarians, and, if that was the case, someone had better raise the alarm, but, since nobody else seemed interested (having sunk too low), it was up to the Colonel himself.

I suppose the Colonel could always gauge his own worthiness by the present state of his assets, but, lest that seem too cynical, let me hasten to add that there was also something driving the man which most of us lack. The Colonel had a sense of outrage. True, his outrage also happened to make him a lot of money, but that did not diminish the strength of his feeling. It was as if this indignation was pushing him toward his last campaign. He seemed to feel obliged to caution Compton once and forever against the onrushing flood that was fast engulfing it.

Yeats reminds us that an aging man is without dignity unless "soul clap its hands and sing, and louder sing . . ." and, indeed, there was something rather Yeatsian about the Colonel's furies. Not only were things falling apart and the center not holding, but every new day produced a lengthening charge sheet of rape, murder, arson, and glue-sniffing, and if the Colonel's soul never quite sang about these things, it managed to print the details of nearly all of them, except perhaps if the perpetrator was a white man (in which case the crime was often relegated to the back pages of the second section). When he was not praising the late Chief Parker, he was castigating the Earl Warren Court. A special place in hell seemed to be reserved for those who practiced interracial crimes (whites and Negroes who were caught together in any number of socially and morally proscribed acts), and a regular feature on the inside pages of the Colonel's paper, along with reports on Rotary speakers, municipal advertisements, press releases from the California Realtors' Association, was the "Police Blotter"—a twice-weekly chronicle of the minutiae of transactions between the Hub City police and its citizenry, which ranged from myna-bird disappearances to larceny and violence, and in which every act was recorded with the solemnity which Holinshed had reserved for the deaths of princes.

Obviously, then, the reign of the Prince of Darkness was upon the Earth and iniquity was blotting out the sun. Sometimes it seemed as if the Colonel was sorely pressed to know which of his enemies was most deserving of his opprobrium: the civil rights marchers who were copulating on the sneak in Mississippi, or the Castro agents who were about to take over Brazil, the Argentine, Aruba, or Puerto Rico? Strange vicissitudes were besetting the Commonwealth: the hour was short, the need great. Somebody was ruining the dollar. A third force was at work banning school prayers. And a fourth was whispering in Johnson's ear: "We shall overcome!"

And, somehow, it all came to be reflected in what was

taking place on the streets of Compton. Poor Compton—ravished by floods, shaken by temblors, and engulfed by Negroes. In 1888, 1914, 1926, 1938 and 1958, the town had been inundated by tidal waters. In 1933, a quake had sent its buildings crashing down to their foundation stones. Around 1954, the black masses broke through its lily-white precincts. In future, one could expect all the city's septic tanks to shoot up into the air like geysers, and then the walls of the Los Angeles Memorial Mausoleum would crumble like sodden graham crackers releasing the packed pollutions of two decades of highly seasoned corpses on Myrrh and Tamarind, Acacia and Pomegranate Streets. Was the Colonel saying *après moi le déluge?* You bet your sweet life he was!

"Nobody here takes the Colonel that seriously any more," one of the professional social-welfare liberals assured me. I think he was mistaken, and that a great many people of Compton shared that same Hieronymus Bosch vision of things to come. Although Negroes were probably not among them, many Negroes in Compton had been sufficiently terrified by the fires of Watts that they rarely raised objections about the Colonel's good intentions. Nor did one hear so much as a peep out of even the liberals in regard to the Colonel's excesses. Probably, the liberals had been rather more intimidated than they wished to admit by the cries of "Burn, baby, burn!" And, besides, to criticize the Colonel was to criticize one of the few institutions of which Compton could boast. Moreover, so long as he lived and breathed and printed newspapers inside that vacuum, he was still a powerful man, a force to be reckoned with. Rumor had it that if you advertised in any competitive newspaper, the Colonel would simply refuse to accept your ads. It was a fact, however, that the Colonel had a way of making his competitors seem like subversives; if one attempted to lure away some of his lucrative "job printing" business, there might be denunciations in his newspaper of such persons as outsiders, interlopers, carpetbaggers, a ruthless band of adventurers at best, or, at worst, reckless, feckless, and incompetent.

But it was difficult to criticize a man who still put so much passion into his privateering. There was also no denying that the competition really wasn't very much; it was, in fact, hardly even respectable. Of the two other community newspapers serving the Compton area, one was colored a vivid green, like the flat racing edition of the old *San Francisco Chronicle*, and just never seemed to be able to get beyond four pages (one of which was often comprised of a house ad); and the other—a Negro weekly which claimed to serve Compton, Willowbrook, and Enterprise— looked as if it had been set in type by the remedial reading class of a New York City school, and then copyread by the editors of the *Morgen Freiheit*. It was unreadable, and perhaps that was a tragedy for black Compton which only apathy seems to explain.

So outlandishly awful were these two other papers that the Colonel's publication, by contrast, seemed rather urbane, almost sophisticated: eight columns wide and of standard length, the typeface greyed down, the heads black enough, but not so black as to seem funereal, nor ever so big as to be sensational. Upon occasion, the Colonel's paper ran to as much as seventy pages in its two main sections. There was also a week-end entertainment pull-out. Not bad for Compton! The Colonel sometimes ran canned comments from California's right-wing educational gadfly, Dr. Max Rafferty, and from Congressman Clawson. There was an inspirational cartoon strip, a house cartoonist, a sports editor, a real-estate editor, and one or two other columnists of the same order. Sometimes there were even letters to the editor; almost always, these were about how Compton was going downhill. Occasionally, too, certain longish items of natural history would stray into print—say, about the number of eagles hatched in the canyons of the Upper Colorado River, or the abrupt decline in the grunion runs, but what the whole thing hung together on was the Colonel's personality; his wrath was almost palpable. And in between all the epithets about Martin Luther King and the punks at Berkeley, one could find between ten and twenty pages of real-estate advertising, decorated here and there with a shield attesting to the fact that Compton had once been chosen as an All-American City. Somehow, there seemed to be a pay-off to every press release, to every signed column; for the Colonel was constantly being testimonialized by this or that Chamber of Commerce, Lions, or Rotary of South Gate, Lynwood, Lakewood, Paramount, or Bell, or receiving letters from governors, mayors, the heads of large trade associations which he would again, solemnly run as news items among his front pages. It

127

seemed that anything which happened to the Colonel was grist for his newspaper's mill.

During my stay in Compton, I tried on at least six different occasions to make an appointment with the Colonel, only to be told by a man who sounded very much like the tobacco auctioneer L. A. (Speed) Riggs (and who referred to himself as the Colonel's "aide de camp") that it was just not possible—no more than it was possible to read through his morgue or to scrutinize his paid circulation figures. Nothing was ever possible within the Colonel's ranks except when the Colonel said it was, and nowadays the Colonel very seldom made public appearances, except in those photographs on the front page of his newspaper. But, although it seemed that few except for his junior officers saw the Colonel, he still managed to give the illusion that he was seeing everything. I used to leaf through his publication and be continually astonished by the excesses of this man who, along with his regular column, would also take precious newspaper space to report on his recent vacations in Panama or Yucatan, even printing his own blurry snapshots of the locks in the Canal to illustrate such texts. Once when I commented to one Compton man that I didn't give a hoot about how the Colonel felt about the Mayan ruins, he smiled and said, "You may not, but folks here like to read those kind of things. When the Colonel talks about them, they make sense. They know they're not ever going to get to all those places, and having the Colonel there is just about the next best thing."

Then I realized that the Colonel was not, after all, such

a novel figure to find ensconced in a city composed to such a degree of displaced white Southerners and southern Negroes. Not only was he an entirely familiar figure to them culturally, representing all that they might have liked to be, but he seemed to symbolize all that they knew they could never be. His arrogance was the glass through which they judged their own reticence. His temper was the garment of meekness they wore turned inside out. His intolerance was their intimidation, his outspokenness their self-censorship, his success their failure, and his bluster their naïveté. In short, he dared to be all the resentments which they held inside themselves, to act out their prejudices, to tilt at their windmills; and they loved him for it. The Colonel might complain endlessly in his column about the misbehavior of "colored people," the arrogance of the working classes, the aggressiveness of trade unions, or about what inflation was doing to the investments market, and people seemed to take it all in and enjoy it because they, after all, did not commonly enjoy the luxury of such problems, and it was entertaining to have somebody close at hand—a neighbor who could be trusted—who actually did. For, if the Roman mob had loved Coriolanus but demanded his death when he turned arrogant, Compton seemed to love their Colonel more the more he scorned them.

Perhaps this simply indicates the distance western civilization has come from Rome to Compton, but it also reveals the new spirit of tolerance that afflicts the common man. In a drab era, life seemed just a little less gray with the

Colonel standing by to hector you. If one knew that he was really "just plain folks" underneath it all, it became a kind of a game, rather delightful at that. Every time I thought of the Colonel, I was reminded of the Housman poem about the mercenaries "whose shoulders held the sky suspended," but I was instantaneously deflated when I reflected that about all the Colonel seemed to be holding up was his balance sheets. In "the hour when heaven was falling," he had truly sacrificed nothing except, perhaps, a couple of hours during one of his Canal crossings to write one of his columns. So the most exact comparison was to one of those truly upper-class British gentlemen—someone who was not in the least diminished because he had the liberty to express all the resentments, greeds, and prejudices which we underlings almost surely feel but never dare to express.

Or so I thought, until the day when I went again to the Colonel's offices to inquire if I could read through that morgue. This time I was luckier on two accounts: first, I had been given an introduction to one of the staff members who was described to me as a "good guy"; and then, when I reached this fellow's desk, he happened to be talking to the Colonel on the telephone: "Yes sir . . . Colonel . . .

"Yes, Colonel, sir . . .

"Yes sir, Colonel . . ."

Although I couldn't make out a word that the Colonel was saying, I could hear his voice, a low drawl. The sound seemed to throw a Pillsbury caste over his listener's complexion:

"Of course I will, sir . .

"Yes. Of course, sir . . ."

At last, he hung up, this fellow whom I shall call Ronald, and stared at me with a dull, abused look: "What can I do for you?"

I introduced myself, alluding to our mutual acquaintances, and then reminded him of the arrangements which had been made. "Oh sure," Ronald said. "I've been expecting you."

Ronald took me back through the offices to a shed in the rear in which the rotting volumes of old newspapers were lying about in a state of neglect. "Have a good time," he joked, leaving me. Ten minutes later, the same employee who had ejected me on my first visit reappeared. "I thought I told you how the Colonel doesn't like people to read this stuff," he said. He didn't even have to use force. Meekly, I let him lead me a second time out through the establishment.

But, as soon as I got outside, I started to worry about Ronald. Would he be getting into any trouble on my account? When I called him, Ronald seemed very upset. He told me that he had to see me immediately. I started to apologize for having gotten him into any trouble, but Ronald said he wasn't worried about that. If I would meet him in the bar down the block, he said he would explain everything, only he would have to be very careful and circumspect. It might not sit well with the Colonel—his being seen in my company.

Fifteen minutes later, I was lurking in the shadows of an alleyway next to the bar when Ronald appeared, smiling.

"There's no need for that," he insisted quietly, but he led me in through the back entrance of the bar and insisted that we take a seat in the darkest section near the men's room.

"Look," I cautioned him, "I hope you're not doing anything you shouldn't be doing."

"As a matter of fact, I am," Ronald said, turning rather waspish, "but now that we're in this together . . ."

"In what?"

Ronald wouldn't answer me directly, but that faint smile seemed to hint that he would explain everything. Then he started to describe what an extraordinary man the Colonel was, how he was not to be tampered with. "I've only been here four months," Ronald said, "but I'll tell you this much: the Colonel is a man of great power and mystery. Some day I'm going to write a novel about him. That's the only reason why I hang around. I'm going to get to know all about that old man, and then I'm going to write a big fat novel about him. You think I would be sitting here in Compton for any other reason?"

Ronald was staring at me aggressively, but all he did was answer my tentative smile with his smile, and then he added: "It isn't that I have any more respect for the man's ideas than you do, but I don't think you ought to mess around with him. He's just too powerful, and I wouldn't like to see anything happen."

Which was an unusual remark to make, because the Colonel and I hadn't even been properly introduced, but when I assured Ronald that I wasn't planning "to mess around" with him, was only hoping to inquire what part, if any, the Colonel had played in Compton's civic life, he glared at me imperiously: "I could tell you things . . . Sure I could. But I think I'll just save it. You know what I happen to think? I'm going to put it in a novel some day. What do you think of that?"

It didn't matter what I thought. The awe which his ambitions had inspired in Ronald's own breast was so swollen that, as he proceeded to talk further, Ronald suddenly felt the need to glance about the darkened lounge, just to reassure himself that he wasn't being spied upon.

"I must be getting back," he interrupted himself. "I can't take any chances."

He dropped some change on the table and started to leave. Then he was back again, bending over the table, whispering at me: "Are you free tonight?"

I was so startled that I said yes without thinking.

"Jesus. That's just great," Ronald said. "There's this gal I'd like you to meet."

"I'm a married man," I confessed, somewhat disconsolately.

"It isn't like that." Ronald was waving away some smoke from his eyes. "She's on the paper. She works for the Colonel. She's going to be at my house tonight. Here's the address. You be there about 8:30." He handed me a slip of paper and disappeared into the shadows.

Ronald's flat turned out to be in a dingy older section of town which consisted of tree-lined streets with paint-flaked houses, front porches, even gliders. For a moment, I thought I was back in Brooklyn, but the air was bitter with the stench of a nearby petroleum cracker, and the night sky overhead was still bruised with the remains of the day's smog. The address Ronald had given me was for a two-story stucco building with twin glass-paned entrances up at the top of some steps which flattened out from a red concrete stoop. When I parked the car and went up to ring his doorbell, the upstairs flat seemed to go all black. Downstairs, however, the lights were blazing, and there were two small children doing somersaults in a tiny front parlor, while a TV blared, under the supervision of a Negro maid in a white uniform. I rang Ronald's bell a second time, but again there was no answer. So I sat on the stoop, smoking. Presently, the downstairs maid stuck her head through one of the open front windows: "Who you looking for?"

I explained that I had been invited by the people upstairs. "They ain't here," she said. "Drove away half an hour ago."

I looked at my watch. It was now well past the hour when I was expected. "I guess they'll be back any minute," I said.

The woman smiled: "Suit yourself, baby," shutting the window tight.

When Ronald still didn't appear within the next half hour, I decided to wait another ten minutes and then call the offices of the newspaper. I called. There was no answer. I called Ronald's home number and got a busy signal. Then I checked with the operator. The phone was off the hook.

I wrote a note to Ronald which explained I had been there, had waited, and was now going, and I made sure to scribble my telephone number on it before dropping it into his mailbox, then drove back toward Noni's. At the Sycamore, Noni told me there hadn't been any calls. I instructed Noni that I planned to be up for a while, and then I went into my room and started to transcribe some notes.

At about 11:30 the phone rang.

"I'm sorry about not making it tonight," Ronald lied, as soon as Noni handed me the phone. "I had a lot of dark-room work to do. Just couldn't be helped."

Yet it was obvious from the tone Ronald used that he was just a little ill-at-ease. He actually seemed to be cautioning me not to question him too severely, or he, in turn, would be obliged to compound this lie with still another. I said: "OK, Ronald, maybe we can make it some other night."

"Maybe so," he said.

I said then: "I guess you wouldn't want to tell me how I can get in touch with that girl."

"I guess not," Ronald said. Clearly, somebody had been busy aggravating his already advanced case of Colonel-phobia, perhaps even the Colonel himself, for he added: "You understand. Sometimes when you get so busy you just lose all sense of time."

I said of course I understood. But I added again that I would like to learn more about the Colonel.

"Yes," Ronald flatly replied, "I just bet you would." He didn't even bother to say good-bye. He hung up.

And that was almost the last I saw of Ronald, the last serious effort I made to find out what I could about the Colonel. I was just afraid that if I persisted, my sense of frustration would grow, and I would become as angry as the old man himself. Besides, I felt that I already knew a good deal more than I wanted to know. But, about one week later, I brushed against Ronald at a city council meeting: "How's the Colonel these days?"

"There are some things," Ronald said, ill-at-ease once again, "which I don't joke about." He ducked inside a telephone booth to call the paper.

· · ·

This is a story which lacks an ending. At last report, the Colonel was alive and well, and Ronald was still hoping to write a novel about him some day. If he plays his cards right, he may also end up as the Colonel's successor and then, probably, there won't have to be any novels.

Pity poor Compton all the more: ravished by floods, shaken by temblors, engulfed by Negroes, and left to the likes of Ronald.

2

CHAPTER VIII

COMPTON VIEWS ITSELF

T he longer I stayed in Compton, the more aware I became that the citizenry had distinct opinions about what was happening to their community. These were not so well focused that they tallied with the views of those professionals and elitists of other sorts whose opinions seem to prevail in the various social analyses that are always being put forward to alleviate this problem or to mitigate that one, but such views were often finely attuned to people's own conditions and sensitive as a wound even when, unfortunately, irrelevant to their immediate conditions. The sociologists talked of anomie, but most residents of Compton still thought it of some importance that they lived in a place called Compton. Most thought they had chosen to move there, and they had very definite ideas about their neighbors, their children's future lives, their responsibilities, their inclinations. Again, very little of this sensitivity seemed to intrude upon the sociological reports drawn from questionnaires through which agencies like the Welfare Planning Council of California* sought to resolve problems in such an area. Here then is Compton as seen by a portion of its citizenry.

NONI:

That isn't my real name. On the street where I grew up there was this bigger girl. She always used to carry me to church, to the store, to pick berries. Sometimes I liked it, but sometimes I didn't, so I used to say, "No . . . no . . . no . . ." Pretty soon they started calling me Noni. Actually my mother called me Edna and my twin sister Ella. Ella died when I was two.

My mother was a Bolivar. They had some Indian and some white blood in them. People said they were from Louisiana. My Aunt Tuni said the Bolivars were freemen. My mother was real light. So was Aunt Tuni. Only father was a blackman. His name was Ezra Walker and he had a cork leg. He lost it hitching a freight during the First World War. Everybody where we lived knew my father because of that cork leg, and most everybody respected him. He dug coal, and he supported us all real well. There were eight children, not counting Ella. I was third from the oldest. I went to work when I was thirteen. We just needed the extra money. But when my father was alive, we did real

* See their interesting but rather too-schematized report: "Compton: A Community In Transition," by David Franklin, Welfare Planning Council of Los Angeles, January, 1962.

good. It was the war. He worked for a white man, a small contractor. My father was strong. Real strong! Some weeks he would earn as much as $135 digging coal, and in those days in Alabama that was a lot of money. Negroes couldn't join unions, so my father worked in the scare mines where the unions wouldn't work. That's how he died. Coal seam caved in. He was dead before they could get to him. Well this man, the contractor, lied about how much he was paying my father, so the Workmen's Compensation didn't give us next to anything. There was just the house, but no savings. The relatives helped a little. My mother went to work, and we older girls did a little. After a while, she went to the County.

In those days, a colored person could only get surplus foods from the County, but no money for rent or food or clothing. Father being a hard-working man, we never had eaten that way, and my mother was ashamed to start now. She used to make us boiled food and soul food. She wouldn't use what the County gave her. And she didn't like the social workers. I guess I was fourteen when Aunt Tuni got me that job with the Biber family. I was supposed to look after the children and help with the serving. They paid me five dollars a week, but when the old colored woman didn't show up, I had to cook and clean for all of them too.

My father wanted me to be a nurse. Seemed like there would be no chance of that if I stayed at Bibers', so when I was fifteen I went to my Uncle Bolivar's place in Biloxi. He said he would send me through high school so I could get up in the world. Well, I hadn't been inside school for nearly a year and I guess I'd just grown up too much at Biber's. After a while, I got bored and went back to my people. My sisters were growing up. My oldest brother, George, was in the Air Force. Momma was working days for a white family out near Bessemer. Somebody had to look after the house, so I stayed home and raised my little sister and made lunches for the other children and did their cleaning and housework.

I didn't really mind it because, in those days, I was young and strong and I didn't have anything else to do. But when I got to be maybe eighteen, I felt restless again. It just wasn't enough taking care of the house like that. I wanted to meet people. Momma always said, "Noni, I want you to promise me you'll be a decent girl," but she wasn't strict in the wrong ways. When I met Blake, she understood.

I don't know why I picked Blake, except that he used to hang around a lot and he was built good, just like my father. Also he had a gentle smile. Some of the colored men where I lived were real sporting, but Blake seemed shy, although he knew all about women. One night he asked me to take a walk. We went out beyond the hills to where we could see the glowing of those furnaces. Blake said he noticed me a long time ago. He asked would I go to the movies with him next week. My brother Bill said, "What do you know about this boy?" But I went anyway. Seems like we just stayed together from that day on. I mean, we clicked, that's all . . .

Blake is from Hampton Roads, Virginia. He came to

Birmingham to work in the mills, but he never could find anything steady. He was always getting sick. If you were to look at him, you would say Blake's well-built and he would be very flattered, but he wasn't fed the right things when he was young, and he isn't all that strong. When Blake came to stay I used to make him stews and greens and he put on a lot of weight. Pretty soon, Blake was so strong that he started talking about California. He said there was work for everybody out here. Well, I believed him, but I didn't want to travel with a little baby. Then we had another baby and another. After a while I put a stop to that. But there never seemed to be enough money and, pretty soon, Blake was working at whatever he could get. One day I saw how narrow he was starting to look. I said, "All right honey, if you think you got a chance there we'll just arrange to do it." I didn't want to leave my family and I missed Birmingham, but I didn't want Blake to get bitter and turn sporting. We came out here in a 1946 Ford with fifty dollars. That was two years ago. Now Blake's in the union. We haven't done too bad.

Blake likes it here because he likes to fish. He likes the outdoor life. He doesn't like to chase after other women, and he's not always in the bars. That's what I was afraid of when I got here, but Blake never was that way. He wanted us to come here for the sake of the children and I suppose he's right. They going to an all-black school here just like in Birmingham, but maybe it's a little better.

You want to know the difference between this place and Birmingham? It isn't all that different. Here the white man smiles at you, and then he hates you just as much behind your back. In Birmingham it was all out in the open. You know you got to bow and scrape a little for the white folks, but you also get your hand in once in a while.

Folks work much harder here too. Seems like they don't like to take it easy. In Birmingham nobody was a bum, but we had neighbors and we used to visit with them all the time. Life was cheaper in Birmingham, so you didn't have to work so hard. And the men were sporting, but they minded their wives. Here a man gets a little money in his pocket and he goes wild. In Birmingham we didn't let people get that far out of line. The girls were all decent and the men were true to their wives, even if they took their pleasure elsewhere.

In Birmingham there wasn't all this trouble with the police, too. When a boy stepped out of line, Minister spoke to his family and they minded him. It isn't like that here. Nobody minds anybody because nobody knows anybody that well. In Birmingham we were poor and they gave us the worst schools and the worst parks, but we fixed them up a little. Pretty soon, they were so nice even the white people got jealous. They took one park away from us. That's the difference. They would never do that here. I doubt if they could do that here.

In Birmingham you treated the white man like a boss and then laughed behind his back. Plenty of white men had Negro women, but you didn't talk about it in public. A girl who did those kind of things, she wasn't thought very highly. But we didn't hold it against the white men all the same. Some really liked their Negro women. It was just as hard for some of them, believe me.

All in all, I like Birmingham better than this place, but Blake is right. There are more opportunities here. And you do got to think of your kids. Blake and I figure we'll stay here maybe another couple of years. By then we should have the money saved to buy our own house. I suppose we could buy one now like so many colored people do with no money down, but we don't want to owe anybody all that money. Blake has a good job and they like him there. Still, who knows what can happen? I remember what it was like for my mother.

Sometimes I get homesick for Birmingham even now, especially when I have to stay up so late and work so hard. That's why I'll be glad to see my sister and her husband. They have seven kids, and a couple weeks ago they just picked up everything and started out here. My brother-in-law said he was just fed up. In the Army he was a mechanic. Down there he had to hustle for every cent. He was always outsmarting the white man. But it wasn't such an easy life. My brother-in-law is even smarter than Blake. He knows how to make gardens and lay field stone. He's a good carpenter, and he can sell. Sometimes I think he may be just too smart. I mean him chucking up everything, the house he built and everything, to come out here. He's going to have to work just as hard. And how does he know what he'll get? Blake's trying to fix him up with something at the

145

factory in the meantime. That isn't his kind of work. If he were a white man, he would be a businessman. He's no fool, my brother-in-law.

The truth is, none of us were down there in Birmingham. You think just because we didn't have proper schooling, we didn't know anything. I learned by watching other people, and I always tried to be decent. I'd like my kids to get all the schooling they can stand, but I wouldn't like them to turn snooty on Blake and me. The truth is I used to read a lot myself. At Bibers' there were always books lying around and I used to glance at them. Then, whenever I had the money, I would buy a magazine. I knew you were a writer the moment I saw you. Why? Because you have such a smart face. I bet I read some of your things in *Cavalier*. Blake sometimes gets that magazine at the factory.

FLORITA:
I have only two children. My sister—who lives not so far away—she has three, and they are a little older than mine. So if I think the Welfare is coming to see me, I tell Rita to bring her children to me. The Welfare comes. They talk to the children. They pay me for all five . . . And when they are going to see Rita, I send her my children in the same way. We don't like to do these things, but we have to live.

And I worry all the time that they will talk to the neighbors, and they will learn the truth, but there is nothing I can do about that now. The neighbors have to be trusted.

A few are on the Welfare just like me. I think they have things they are hiding too.

For example, I know that the woman in the big house down the block is not so sick as people say she is. That woman, she gets a big pension for the eyes because they say she can't read so good any more, but I have seen her with the newspaper. I have seen her with her husband at the TV. Who cares? If she is getting more than she should get, it is her good fortune. I would never say a word. I don't want her to say anything about me and my children.

When the social workers used to be in Bell, they told me that I should think about going to live with my sister in a great big house because it would mean that we would be able to help each other and we could live much better, but I said, "I don't get along so well with her." Believe me, I was terrified. I said, "She and I . . . we are not of same mother . . . not of the same blood." Those social workers wouldn't leave me alone until they had a chance to talk with both of us all together. So Rita knew what to do. She said, "I hate that bitch Florita because she went off with my boyfriend . . ." And the social workers shook their heads and didn't bother us again.

If you want to know if what Rita said is true, I shall have to tell you it is not, but there is a fact that this boy I knew was Rita's even before he was mine. I don't think she hates me because of that. She would be silly if she did. Because that boy isn't here any more . . . and she knows it.

You ask me about the future, but I am not going to tell

147

you all kinds of lies about how wonderful it is for me, and I am not going to say it is terrible. It is what it is; it could be a lot worse. I live here because the schools are good and I want my children to have the education. When they are older, I will look for work. If the children do well in school, it will be better for all of us, better for them to have the education, and better for me to have them to look after me. Now, all I have is the Welfare, and it comes and it goes. Even with Rita's children, it isn't what it should be. But I am a good manager.

JACK WHITE:

I'm here to help the kids without fathers. They need a man like me to talk to. I don't say I know as much as a lot of other people, but I know things. I've lived. When I was sixteen, I did spot welding for Henry Kaiser. That's how I got to California, through Henry Kaiser.

Henry Kaiser was building ships in Richmond. I was in Newport News, but they wouldn't hire any Negroes in the yards down there. Then the government said you got to do it, and I went down to the yards with this friend of mine, but we were just too late. "There isn't anything here," the hiring boss said, "but if you'll go to California, we'll pay your fare and I promise you a year's work." I had no family except my mother, so I came out here. I've been here ever since.

It wasn't easy in the beginning, because even the unions were Jim Crow and they managed to make the scale different for us and the white workers. We couldn't even find any place to live. There were always fights. If a Negro went into a bar they would say: "What you doing here, Jiggaboo?" And, of course, the women were off limits.

I worked at Kaiser till the end of the war, and I saved about four thousand dollars. By then the Communists were in our union and they were pretty much running things. They sort of catered to Negroes. They sent me to the California Labor School. They gave me lots of books to read. I figured they were just like all the others when you got right down to what they were really like. I mean, when things started getting hot for them, they turned bigot and forgot all about us. In 1947, I went up to Seattle looking for work in the aircraft plants.

Well, because of my going to that California Labor School they wouldn't take me on anywhere, but, by then, old Truman did away with the Jim Crow, and I went with some friends of mine and joined up. They sent me to Fort Lewis, but when I told them I could spot weld, they asked if I wanted to go to Germany. I never had been overseas and I thought the color problem would be better in Europe, so I said sure and they shipped me out right after advanced training. For two years I was in the Black Forest near Stuttgart. We called the place Kaiserslautern. I liked that place. I don't know whether you would or not.

I say that because I know you're a Jew and even in those days there was a lot of anti-Semitism over there. But it was different for us. We had to maintain the equipment, and they treated us good. The German girls didn't seem to care. We were their protectors from the Russians. I learned a

149

little Deutsch when I was in Kaiserslautern. "Machs nix" and "voss is loss." Some other words too. When my time was up, I honestly thought of staying on, but this friend of mine, Peter Higgins, said, "You don't owe Mr. Truman anything, and he don't owe you anything. If you stay on, they'll get rid of you sooner or later," because they were dropping out a lot of men before their twenty years were up, "so you ought to go out and get yourself fixed in civilian life before it's too late. After all," Pete said, "you ain't getting any younger."

Pete Higgins had a sister lived in Watts. After our discharges we went to stay with her. It wasn't a good time. The aircraft factories were slumping, now that Korea was over, and the whites got all the best jobs. Peter and I still had about three thousand dollars in discharge pay between us, so we thought we'd open up a little business. You know? A service station? Mechanical things. Gas, oil. You can make a living if you got the right franchise, but all we could get was Star Gas—they're no longer in business—and everybody complained it knocked like hell.

The truth is it was just as good as Calso or Esso only the mark-up was much smaller, and with all that talk about what it did to your motors, business kept dropping off. One week was worse than the one before. Pretty soon there wasn't enough for Pete and me, so I said, "You can have the place. I'll find something else to do."

Pete's still got the place, too, only he doesn't sell gas. He does a little body work. Sells retreads. It doesn't amount to a hell of a lot. I don't begrudge him it either. I'm just glad my name wasn't on any of the notes, because he'll have to pay for them the rest of his life. The truth is that Star Gas was a racket. Pete got stuck. Not those other guys. They were a corporation, and they just disappeared from the face of the earth, but Pete couldn't run and hide anywhere. It was hard enough with just the two of us making a go of that thing. Then he got married. He had three kids. His oldest boy helps out after school. I don't envy Pete.

If we're still friends, it's because of his sister Mary. She is a wonderful girl. Every Christmas she has the gang of us for dinner. She's a marvelous cook. Her husband works in the post office, and they're just about getting by, but they always set an extra plate at the table.

Mary and I kept company for nearly three years. It was just like being married. Mary was a sleep-in for a family in Santa Monica, but she came home to stay with me weekends. I'm not ashamed of it. We lived together as man and wife. Her husband knows that. If it weren't for what happened with the business, we probably would have gotten married, but when we near went broke, I said, "It wouldn't be right." And I went away for nearly a year.

By the time I came back, Mary was married. I wasn't bitter. I bought them a set of dishes. I felt I should, so there would be no hard feelings, and whenever I come to dinner they put those dishes out on the table. Anyway, I guess I was meant to be a loser. I couldn't have made Mary happy. I'm just a difficult person sometimes. When I went off that time by myself, some people thought I was in jail, that I'd never come back, but I just wanted to be by myself. I had a little car and maybe a couple of hundred dollars. I drove right straight up the coast highway. Occasionally I would come to a little town and do chores for a few days to keep me in spending money. I slept out by the car in an old sleeping bag. It was a good feeling.

By late spring, I was in Fairbanks, Alaska. I had read in this magazine that they wanted workers and were willing to pay a lot of money. It was easy to get a job. First, I worked in construction. Then I got a mechanic's job at a bus depot. The money was good, too. Sometimes I made three hundred dollars a week. But I never kept much of it. For one thing, I took to drinking quite a bit. Then, too, I was lonely. But I believe the real reason was the segregation. I had to pay two hundred dollars a month for my room and board with this colored family. It's the same all over. Most colored people don't own anything, and they get stuck for a lot of money when they do.

In 1958, I came back to Watts. My thought was to go out to Kern County and get in on that oil boom, but Mary's husband, Graham, said, "That isn't a place for a colored man. That's all redneck out there." Well, I had a little money saved up and a lot of big ideas, and I just wouldn't take no for an answer, so I drove to Bakersfield. I'll never forget it. It must have been 110 in the shade. I was broiling alive. Graham said he knew a Chinaman there with a colored wife from Watts. He told me to look them up. I guess I never did. My very first night in town I went to this bar for a cold beer and a white guy said to me, "Something stinks in here!

"Say," he announced, "anybody else smell that stink?"

Well I knew what he was getting at, but I was trying to play dumb. I just sat and drank my beer. I even ordered another. The next thing I knew I heard another white voice: "Nigger, I got your number. You get up out of that stool, leave your money on the bar, and walk on out of here."

"I ain't bothering anybody," I said.

The next thing I knew I was in the county hospital with my skull split down the middle. I guess they thought I was going to be biggity. I still got a crease in my head. Police said I was lucky to be alive. Sure, they took me down to headquarters when I was up and around again and asked whether I would identify the guys. I knew they didn't mean it. As soon as that doctor said, "Go on home," I beat it.

Where did I go? Back to Willowbrook again. I knew old Graham would say, "I told you so," but it was the closest thing I had to home, and I've been here ever since. I haven't any complaints. I'm good with my hands. I can always make a living. Most of the time I just do odd jobs, repair things, do a little plastering and painting and roofing. Sometimes, I'll take a regular job, like in a factory. I don't like to stay if I can help it. For one thing, you stay around and they giving you a little bit more and you're spending a little bit more and pretty soon they got you. You're just no good to anybody then. And if you get too ambitious, you'll also be sorry. So I work at different things. I do repairs for people around here when something gets all busted up, like a car; and I do chauffeuring, if somebody has to get some place. I even do a little gardening.

It got so everybody around Willowbrook knew I was just the guy they could come to when they needed something mechanical fixed up, and I had a lot of kids hanging around. Those kids . . . they had nothing to do and nowhere to go except trouble. They just used to hang around. Pretty soon I started teaching them little things: how to grease a car, the different types of wrenches, that sort of thing. Some of them got pretty handy, and they would help me. We would do a job together and I would pay them. I didn't know they were playing truant, but it didn't matter. If they would teach those things in school, they wouldn't need people like me. Well, anyway, when the poverty program started, the people said, "Jack, they ought to give you some work," and they did, but I didn't get along with the social workers. Then I rented this place and started charging some of the kids to teach them spot welding and things like that. It wasn't their money I wanted. I just thought if they had to pay, they would take things more seriously. One of my kids was just out of the service and he had the G.I. Bill. When he told them where he was studying, they said I didn't have the right. Maybe I didn't, but I think I helped a lot of people. So I went back to fixing again, and now I only do the other stuff as a sideline. I let the kids hang around. I guess it's because they don't have fathers.

I think the real reason why people got after me about that school is because I'm a Muslim. It's not a religious thing with me. I don't even like their newspaper. But I think the colored races have got to stick together and that's what Elijah Muhammad means to me. He means strength through power. To me that's all important. When I grew up in Virginia, if a colored man could do something well he did it for the white man, and we never saw him again. He just disappeared up North somewhere. Well, Elijah Muhammad says we're all we got. He teaches that to us. I believe it too because the white man isn't going to look out for us. Take Compton, for instance. All the colored there are busy electing white folks to jobs, and they expect to be thanked for it. Well, all the white man does is say, "Behave yourself." That's why we got to do it our way with our people. It doesn't even have anything to do with race. I just know if we don't get a move on, it's going to get worse before it gets any better. That's my story. That's what I try to teach these kids. If they had fathers, they wouldn't need me. It so happens they don't. Well, it serves the white man right.

MR. BURNSIDE:
The majority of the colored people want everything given to them and they give nothing in return. They are in most cases lazy. The government is afraid of them and is now taking the rights of all the people away to help the colored. But they are taking the rights away from the colored, too, except these aren't enforced. Only the ones against the white man are enforced.

Compton used to be a good place, but it isn't any more.

155

The colored person doesn't accept law and order at all. He wants everything his way. People here are afraid to stand up for their rights because the colored people might riot again. So it's getting worse. As the Negro is starting to take over the community, it's getting to look like a pig pen.

Let's not forget. The negro is a minority group in the U.S., and if the white man acted the way the colored people do, there would be no Negro today. Look. I don't say treat them badly. They ought to be treated just like everybody else. Only they ought to know that white people have rights too. I've been working five years in the same office. I'm called manager. So the other day they brought in this bright kid from Compton Junior College.

DOLLY AND REX:

"Would you believe niggers?" the man said.

And his wife echoed him: "Would you *believe* it?"

We were sitting in a barbecue stand along the Long Beach Road. The tall, lean man with the wasted face was chef. His wife was the waitress. But they didn't own the place. They just worked there and were anxious to chuck it and move on to someplace else, as they had already moved from Upper Michigan to Miami, Florida, and from Florida to Phoenix and now to Compton. They were, in fact, of that new breed of Americans who own nothing and wander, living in motel rooms, driving convertibles, and serving the equally rootless technocratic and semiprofessional classes. The evening before, in a bar, the man had told me how he and his wife had always worked in and around defense industry: at Cocoa Beach, at Vandenberg Air Force Base, because the money was freer with such people, but sometimes they got stuck—like they were now—in a place like Compton. It wasn't quite what they wanted out of life. Their apartment was furnished badly. The swimming pool wasn't heated. And the other day, a Negro and his wife had come to rent rooms. "He said he was some kind of minister," the man said.

"Would you believe it?" his wife put in.

"He didn't look like a bad sort to me," the man said. "The only thing is I don't see why I have to put up with a thing like that. It's bad enough having to wait on them. Would you believe it?" he said. "He came up to my wife and said, 'How dya do. I'm your new neighbor.'"

"Not for long, he is," the wife said. "Would you believe it?"

I found myself believing every word of it. The evening before, at a bar, this young man and his wife had stopped by for one drink and had gone home plastered, giggling: "I hope there's a coon in the back yard. I'd like to shoot me a coon." And when, by accident, I had dropped in that next day to have a bite of lunch and saw them behind the counter, they seemed entirely unself-conscious about what had taken place. "Would you believe it?" the fellow greeted me. "I make the best barbecue in these parts. I use only prime meats, and I don't use hickory powder but the real chips. What will it be—pork or beef? You just take a seat and I'll bring it to you . . . Hey Dolly, show the man where to sit."

157

"Would you believe it?" Dolly said, emerging from the kitchen. She took me by the hand and led me over to one of the booths. Then she asked, "So? You came looking for us?"

"I just happened to be passing by."

"Would you believe it?" Dolly called. "He just happened to be passing by? What'll it be—pork or beef?"

I ordered pork, and a cup of tea with lemon to help cut the fat. When Dolly returned a minute later with my place mat, I said, "Nice place you got here."

"We won't be here very long," Dolly said.

"Where do you think you'll be going?"

"One thing is true," Dolly smiled, "anything would be better than Compton."

"What's wrong with Compton?"

Dolly leaned over with a conspiratorial smile on her face: "It's too close to Watts."

"Now Dolly, I don't like to hear you talking that way in front of the guests." The husband had suddenly appeared by her side with my plate of pork in his hand. He dropped the plate on my mat, and then he and Dolly just stood over me, as if they were going to watch me eat.

"You oughtn't to say such things," the fellow was smiling. "This fellow is from New York. He won't like that kind of talk. Besides," he added, "it isn't Watts. It's Compton. If the niggers really want it that bad, I say give it to them. So Dolly and me will just have to wander off someplace else. It's not the first time. I don't want to get stuck and raise a bunch of kids in one of these places anyway. Give it to them, I say, because it's just about all they're good for."

Rex, for that was his name, realized that he was not quite making the impression that he had hoped to make, so he wiped his hands against his apron and said, "I got a joke to tell you . . ."

"Tell about it," Dolly smiled.

Rex came closer: "Would you like to hear a joke?"

I said, "Why not?"

"Seems there was this Jewish guy," Rex began. "No. Go on ahead. Eat your food. I'll tell you my little joke—

"There was this Jewish guy and every time he made love to his wife she made him put a quarter in her piggy bank.

"Well anyhow, they got to be real old . . . and one night they're lying in bed together and the Jewish guy says, 'Heya Rosa, how about it?'

"And she says, 'Wella Sammy . . . I don'ta know . . .'

"Sounds like they're talking Italian," I said.

"Would you believe it ?"went Dolly.

And Rex said, "I guess you wouldn't like the story anyway. Finish up, mister, and Dolly will give you some pie!"

TENSON:

Melvin Tenson is one of Compton's leading attorneys. One of his partners is a high public official. His wife is a professional social-service employee. They live in a comfortable house in an integrated area of town and have a week-end retreat on the other side of the San Bernardino hills.

159

Tenson is still a young man, hardly more than 45. A combat veteran of World War II, he moved to the West Coast from a small Kansas town shortly after the war, studied law there under the G.I. Bill, and has been an active member of the bar ever since. Like many professionals of his age and generation, Tenson has become a troubled liberal. On the question of "human relations"— Compton's euphemism for the race issue—he remains impeccably liberal and earnest (and he has served on various community boards, was in the forefront of the early efforts to break the color bar in Compton, and has supported a wide range of liberal and reformist causes of value to the Negro community without alienating himself from his fellow white professionals, most of whom are more conservative), but Tenson, like many such liberals, reserves the right to be critical of Negro excesses and stridency, to resent what he regards as bullying; and he seems to feel that Compton Negroes have often "taken advantage" of their burgeoning equality. He keeps finding himself wishing that they would act "more responsibly," keeps restraining himself from apologizing for the excesses of Negro crime and family breakdown. It is as if he were rather disappointed in those whose cause he had once championed. He cannot, for example, comprehend why so many Negro women are on Welfare, while he seems to be having such a hard time finding "decent office help."

"I pay a legal stenographer $150 a week, if she's any good at all," Tenson explains, "and do you know I can't seem to keep one for more than three or four months before I have

to fire them or they quit for something better? I don't
understand it. $150 a week is good money, and they have
fringe benefits: Kaiser Medical Insurance, even profit-sharing after a while. But nothing seems to encourage initiative.
When we had white girls, they would all quit if we hired a
Negro. Now we have Negro girls, and they aren't that much
better. They do as little work as they can, and they're always calling in sick. It's not that I want them to work as
hard as I work, but there has got to be a limit. They're
supposed to be here at 9; they come in at 9:30. They bring
coffee and a Danish pastry, too, so it's nearly ten before
they start typing. Then they take an hour's lunch and they
shop or meet their girl friends. They never seem to eat
lunch, because they usually come back with a little bag
with a sandwich in it. So it's 2:30 before they are back at
work again, and then they want to get out of here at 5 sharp
to meet their boy friends, even if I want to pay them over-
time . . .

"I just can't understand," Tenson continues. "I don't
expect them to do anything I wouldn't do, but I can't even
get them to keep up. White or colored . . . it doesn't
seem to matter. They're on the phone all day long with
their girl friends, and they resent it when I mention that
there shouldn't be personal calls. Well, I mean I don't
want to be a son-of-a-bitch, but there has to be a limit.
What they don't seem to realize is they're killing the goose
that laid the golden egg. Then my clients complain that the
work isn't getting out and they end up going someplace else
. . . and then where are we?

"That's why I started the profit-sharing plan, and I even offered to take one girl, who had been with us quite a while, in on a few of our investments. It didn't really help. None of the girls are around that long to share in profits. One girl got tired of this place and went off to San Francisco. In fact, it was rather unpleasant in the end because we had to buy her up, and it wasn't exactly a good time for any of us.

"But don't get me wrong. I'm glad I did the things I did, and I'd like to do even more, if only somebody would show some interest. They just don't. When I was a young man, a girl who worked in an office knew more about some things than the boss, but none of these girls seem to want to learn anything. With them, it's all fun and high living. If I had young lawyers around here, my friends say it would be different, because the girls would want to be nice for the younger men, but I'm not running a dating bureau. I can't worry about their sex lives. They can do what they want. All I want them to do is work. And I don't like it when they waste things. Girls today are terribly wasteful. Typewriters never seem to last. Stuff gets broken or thrown out. They don't seem to care. Let the boss pay. And if you tell them you don't want to be a boss, they act as if they still don't understand. Honestly, sometimes I wonder why I'm in this business. I ought to go to work for somebody else. I'd do just about as well, and I wouldn't have all these headaches . . .

"I've thought a lot about what this all means," Tenson continues, "and I still don't know any of the answers. It used to be a girl would look upon a job like this as part of her life. Now it's just something that you get done so you can go off to Redondo for the evening. Well, I try to understand, but it never seems to mean anything. What's there to understand? These girls say they need to work, but they never have a penny. They dress better than my wife, and they can get very fresh. It's hard enough understanding the woman you live with, but it's even harder dealing with the problems of these girls. They don't seem to have anything tying them down anywhere. They go to Europe on vacation and they eat out at Perrini's. It took me years before I could do anything like that, and these secretaries do it all they like. Well, how can I compete with that? I could pay more money, but where will it end? Somehow I think we've just got to get off this fun splurge and get down to work, but how am I going to make them understand any of that? They just don't agree. They think I want to exploit them. I never exploited anybody in my life. I just want an honest day's work for a good day's pay, but try to make *them* understand. I remember there was this one girl. She used to get sick every month for a few days. I thought it was her women's problems. You know. Then I asked my wife, and she said it isn't anything like that. She said she probably was just taking advantage. So one day, when she came in looking very tan, I confronted her. 'Joyce,' I said, 'if the job doesn't suit you, why not go someplace else. It just isn't right, your doing what you've been doing.' Do you know something? She didn't even answer me. She said

163

she was busy on something, and the next week she asked for her vacation, and when she came back she quit for something better. Very nice . . .

"Honestly, I don't like to complain, but what am I to make of such behavior? All I ask is decency, and I'm not getting it. They take advantage of any chance they can get. It's as if I exploited them. I'd like to know how, at $150 a week. Do you know that's more than I earned in 1952? And I lived and I worked . . . I guess it's different with girls. It's like that with my own daughter. She does as little as she can in school, and when you ask her why, she says, 'I don't have a thing to worry about.'

"So that's why," Tenson concluded, "I find myself getting bitter sometimes. It's not that I don't respect my employees. I would like to, and they don't give me a chance. All they want is the easy way out, and meanwhile I have to carry the load. Well, when it comes down to that, I get pretty riled up. I'm not working to support a bunch of silly girls so they can have love affairs in Lake Tahoe. Tell me something: Where will it all end?"

BRENDA FOX:
Compton? It's ugly. That's the only way I can describe it. It's such an ugly place. I never understood why it has to be so ugly. Other places aren't. I don't mean places like Beverly Hills or Malibu. You wouldn't expect a place where working people live to be that nice. I don't know what I expected when I first came here, but I felt very trapped. I mean, the ugliness was just unbearable. My

husband didn't seem to mind because he worked all day, but I had to be here. When I started having children, it got very depressing. Then my husband began to stay out late at night. Pretty soon he left me, and now I have the children and I don't care if I never see him again. I work in Douglas during the day as a secretary. In the evenings I help out here at the bar. Why? Because when you have three children in a place like this, you dream of something better. I'm saving my money to buy a place somewhere else. Any place! Maybe along the ocean somewhere . . .

I work hard, yes, but I think I would go crazy if I didn't work. What would I do? The children are in school all day. They come home, and they have homework. I really love my kids, but you just can't spend your whole life playing momma. At Douglas you have a nice atmosphere, and a chance to meet people. Here at the bar you also meet people. I don't mean men. I just mean people. When I was married, I hardly knew a soul in Compton because my husband kept me at home and he was very jealous. Then look what he did. I tell you, I don't care if I never see him again, and I don't even think the kids miss him. My little girl asks for him, but that's different. She's still a little girl. The other two are older. They're more understanding. It's the neighbors I really worry about. They seem to be giving me dirty looks all the time. We're all stuck there on the same block, and I guess many of them remember Pat. They can be funny about it, sometimes.

You ask me why I stayed on here? I told you: it was because I felt trapped. There was the house in my name, and that was about all I had; and I felt—I mean sincerely —that it would be wrong to take the children away. I mean, they had been disturbed too much as it was. So I went to see this marriage counselor—I know it was too late—and I asked what he thought I should do, and he said it would be wrong to take the children away, so here I am. I've often thought of getting out, now that the children are a little older, because of this new element here in town, but where would I go and what would I do? Pat sends me just about enough money to make the mortgage payments on the house, and there's a lot of expense to raising three children. I have to keep up a car. I just can't wear housedresses . . . and I like my children to look decent, too. I wouldn't want people to think that because the father left, the mother is neglecting them.

If this new element gets any worse, I will definitely have to sell the house and maybe I will take an apartment or move to one of those developments in Orange County. I think you know what I mean by this new element. I mean *them*. *They* are taking over the whole town. Their children get all the attention in school. I don't know what to say about *them*. *They* have a right to live, I suppose, but why do they have to push themselves on us? My kids say they are all very dirty. Why don't their mothers take the time to fix them up? They have time enough to sit all night in those bars. The trouble with Compton is it's too close to Watts. It's as simple as that. The place was ugly to begin with, and it's getting uglier. I know. They talk about beautifying the city, and some of them even keep up their houses pretty good, but people don't like living with them, and they've let the whole place go to pot. I know what I'm speaking about. When we first moved here, people had hope. Pat used to work nights at Douglas. During the day he took care of the garden, or we would buy things for the house. Then *they* started pouring in, and he just gave up. I don't think it had anything to do with me. It had to do with them. He saw them taking over everything, and he got wild. He just wanted to get out. Well, I had the children to think about. I just couldn't run away. So he went off with her.

MAYNARD KRAUSS:
You ask about Compton? What's there to say? We've been living here ever since the war. I can't complain about it, although it's changed a lot. And I don't mean the Negroes. A lot of my friends think I mean them all the time, but I don't. They're just trying to get by like everybody else. Even a fool can see that much. But that doesn't mean I have to like everything I see. If I don't like everything, it's not even their fault. It's nobody's fault, I guess. It's just a matter of change. I'll tell you what I mean.

Compton used to be a place where, if a man had a house and a family and a good job, he didn't think too much about anything else. We didn't have any big ideas. We came here and it was a good life. We got on. My kids went to school here. Then they wouldn't live here any more. Nobody does. Nowadays, everybody's got big ideas. A man can't think much of himself unless he does. I worked hard and my wife worked during the war because I was in the service, and we wanted our kids to have everything, but we never dreamed that they might have even more than that. We never dreamed that they would do the things they do.

It's just such a different life. It used to be a man worked hard and owned a house and he thought that was darned good, but now that's changed and you don't see those people any more. Everybody's got so much. Everybody's doing things we never dreamed of doing. Nobody has any time to just sit back and have a glass of beer. Well, it's changed. No use crying. I just don't see why I have to like it. Sure, I admire the ones who get ahead, and I wish mine had done a whole lot better in school, but even not doing so well didn't seem to hurt them that much, and pretty soon they got wise to that . . . and that's what I don't like. They're doing much better than I ever did. They're doing just fine, I guess, and they're able to do things we never did. So what's going to happen? Will my kids feel like me thirty years from now? What does it all mean? My wife says we should be thankful that there are such opportunities for everybody, but I don't see it that way. All I see is a bunch of people telling other people how to lead their lives just because they think they're big successes . . . and nobody is a father and nobody has a son any more. It's changed all right . . . and I don't see why I have to like it.

That don't mean I like the old way all that much. I know it's better this way, and I'm not going to be one of those nuts. When I read about them, the Birchites I mean, I think they're just out of their minds. It won't change no matter what we do. We're just living out our lives from now on in. The others are taking over, and they're smart all right. I can see it in my kids and in my grandchildren. They know all the easy ways . . . and all we have now is the Negroes for company. Well, you can't blame some people for getting bitter, but I don't see what they're going to do about it. There are no kids around here any more, and there are no fathers. I told that to the minister the other day when I went to church . . . but I don't even like to go there that often. Never did. Ministers are all hypocrites. They talk like liberals, and then live pretty fancy off their congregations. Well, I don't think that's such a nice thing . . . and I don't see why I need their advice. I decided long ago that I wasn't going to run anywhere. I'm just going to live here and take my sweet time about dying. Do you think I sound bitter? I don't think so. Wait till you hear my kids some day.

MONTY:
You don't know anything about this place. You don't care to know. These people are cannibals. Look at them! They live off the Welfare. They come in this store, and they buy any shit that has a little shine on it. They got no pride. That's all. And I'm supposed to be a good guy. Why? What for? Who was ever so nice to me? Before these people started coming here, I had a smaller trade, yes, but it wasn't like I felt all the time like I couldn't turn my back on anybody. Now I grow eyes behind my head, and it doesn't do a bit of good. These people don't care. They

don't care for anything and anybody. You see them with their fat cans in shorts and halters, and they sweat so much it's awful. These people stink, that's what they do. They should be ashamed of themselves, the way they live, but they ain't ashamed. They ain't ashamed of anything or anybody. That's the secret of their life.

If I was a nigger, I would do anything rather than take Welfare, but they don't care. They don't care one little bit. They believe it's for them, and they like taking it, and if you offer them work, they got a million excuses why they can't do it, and if you hire them, they are lazy or stupid or both. Why should they work? They got the Welfare. I tell you my customers are a bunch of animals. I'm ashamed to deal with them. So why do I bother? You're a very funny boy.

DENNY ROBBINS:

It seemed like all my life, people were always pushing me: back east my mother, my father, my older brother, who is a doctor, and I just didn't like being pushed that way. I had to go to prep school so I could go to a good college, and I had to go to a good college so I could go to medical school. In my sophomore year at Amherst, I was on the tennis team. I met this older woman. She understood. I mean, she was an understanding person. My parents found out. I was so humiliated . . . and she said it's better this way. We broke up. That's all. Then I decided when the time came I would get as far away from them as possible. I graduated and let myself be drafted. The army sent me out here to Fort Ord for the tennis team, and I've been here ever since.

Only I don't play tennis any more. I mean, not that much. Now that I'm away from all that, it just doesn't seem important. I have a job, and I like the beach a lot. I like to keep my body in good shape, so I press weights, but I don't play tennis. That's an entirely different matter. I just like being left alone. That's why I like it here in Compton. Nobody bothers you. I lead an ordinary life, and I don't feel any pressure. I have my own car. I have a nice hi-fi. I could afford to live some other place, but I don't see what I would gain. The people here are just the kind of people I like. They don't bother me. So I'm here and I'll stay here. Maybe, some day I'll get married. In the meantime, I'm not as unhappy as I used to be. I'm not a big deal, and I don't want to be. Back home in Hartford you just had to be something because you were a Negro, and you had certain chances others didn't have, but here I can do just as I like. It's sort of depressing sometimes, because none of my friends have ever been to college and we don't have too much to talk about, but I decided long ago that that was the way I am. I like to lead a nice quiet life. I like to keep regular hours. I don't like being bothered by things. And I don't like to compete. So here I am. Call me a big flop if you want to. What business is it of yours anyway?

TANNER:

Lowell Brison Tanner is the proprietor of a small chain of retail stores in the Compton-Lynwood area. Whenever lists of prospering Negro merchants are compiled, his name is among them. He started out ten years ago with just one small grocery in the Watts area, and has been on the move ever since. Tanner now owns real estate in the Pacoima section of Pasadena, and maintains a small portfolio of stock with one of the local brokerage firms. He has given over the managing of his grocery business primarily to his brother-in-law, now participates in all manner of civic events, and is the father of two teen-aged boys.

When the rioting broke out in Watts, Tanner took part in organizing a local self-protection group of black and white merchants. They were highly commended by the community for their efforts. For Tanner, the rioting revealed something about Negro and white relationships which even he had long suppressed. He says, "Worse than the burning and killing was all the explaining afterwards. Nobody seemed to want to take the responsibility. My people were putting up a front. The whites were upset. It seemed to be leading us nowhere . . . I mean, how can you justify arson and assault? It's like asking somebody to justify poverty. And the result is things are getting worse, not better. Nobody will take the responsibility for my people, so the business community has lost confidence in this area, and then my people cry prejudice, and where does it get us? I'm not saying it's right or even good, but in the end you have to take care of your own. If we're not prepared to do that, we can't go crying prejudice at the white man. That's why I admire some of the kids with their black power slogans. I know that they sound awful scary sometimes, and

I don't like it when they get so blowy about what happened at Watts, but at least they're willing to recognize where the responsibility lies. They say let's do this by ourselves. Let's get together and not let the white man run the whole world. If they mean by that they're willing to take responsibility, then I'm for them. It can't go on like this. Every year it gets worse and worse. We take over Watts and it's a slum. We come here and it's a mess. Well, it just can't go on like that any more. We've got to say to our own people forget about what the white man is doing to you. Worry about what you're doing to yourselves . . . and I think we've got the resources and the people now to do it . . . *if only some of us will take the responsibility.*"

DAHLIA:

Dahlia Gottlieb is a Jewish housewife who has lived in Compton ever since the war. Now that her children are grown, she works in a mental hygiene clinic to help supplement her husband's earnings as a printer. Dahlia and her husband are used to hard work and unaccustomed to affluence. They live in a modest home in a predominantly Negro section of Compton, and find it extremely pleasant. In fact, they chose to move there. Although the original cost of the house was small, over a decade it has appreciated greatly. Their children's friends are mostly Negro, and they are happy among them. The Gottliebs believe in actually acting out their high-minded liberal principles, and they have never been sorry for their decision to move among the Negroes, rather than into the few blocks of town near the

Jewish Community Center which some people in Compton call "the golden ghetto."

But it wasn't always so easy for the Gottliebs. In the beginning, brokers refused to show them any houses in the Negro section of town. Then Dahlia's husband had some bad business reverses, and she had to go out to work. Dahlia now says she chose the Negro district because that way "I felt I wouldn't have to put up with anti-Semitism," but there was even some of that in the beginning. What saved the Gottliebs, probably, was their lack of snobbery or pretense. They have remained members of the blue-collar class without giving way either to affectation or smugness. In the beginning, Dahlia was an enthusiastic joiner of neighborhood organizations, but she consciously restrained herself from rising to the top. She helped when she could, and spoke as freely as she could. Yet Dahlia is increasingly worried about the lives some of her Negro neighbors and friends are living in Compton.

"The women have been to college," she explains. "But the men are working class. They give everything to their children. They also consume a great deal. You see some of these houses, the lawn is beautiful and the trim is painted shipshape, but they don't even have any furniture. It's expensive being Negro and middle class, and they just don't have the money . . . They like to give their children music lessons and dress them up fine—nicer than I would ever dress my kids . . . They buy all of the best things. I have a neighbor like that. He's a hard-working man, and it all goes to the kids. The other day the truck was outside repossessing his furniture.

"It's a funny thing," Dahlia continued, "Watts hurt us just as bad as it hurt Watts. People here can't get loans. Sears is cracking down on charge accounts. The whites are even more alienated than before. They know they just can't carry on like they used to, but they're afraid to get involved. They were afraid that way even before Watts.

"Of course," she added, "for the genuinely middle-class Negro, Compton is a big step up the ladder. The Human Relations Commission really opened things up for him. He was able to join the Chamber of Commerce, even the Rotary, and he's beginning to have a real place in this town. But the poor are still completely out of it. They don't have any relationship to anybody and nobody seems to be doing that much about it."

BRICE:

Lyman Brice is part Navaho Indian and part Negro. Although extremely light-skinned, he is also a leading member of Compton's Negro community, through his own choice.

Brice works as a salesman in a radio and television outlet. He is married to a white woman and they live in an integrated district of town; and they often attend meetings of the NAACP, the National Council of Negro Women, and the City Human Relations Commission. Brice does all this despite the fact that he claims he has never personally been the target for racial discrimination. In fact, he seems to set himself apart from those Negroes who are its targets, without necessarily lessening his commitment to their well-being. Brice is well respected by the white community but is often accused of being an Uncle Tom by Negroes. That is because he is anxious to work through established political alliances, rather than set up a separate power bloc of his own. Sometimes, Brice seems to be saying that the ghetto Negro is as much a victim of his own self-hate and self-pity as anything else.

"Some people just like to live like pigs in a place like Watts," he will say. But he never follows this line of argument for very long. Ultimately, Brice is quite cognizant of the disabilities resulting from color which are imposed upon the Negro even in Compton. Here, for example, are his views on politics in the town:

"When a white man says of a Negro that he thinks about Compton, not just about those minority groups, he means that this man is willing to put down his own people if he can strike a deal of mutual interest to all.

"When a Negro says of a Negro he's just an Uncle Tom, about the same thing is meant . . .

"When a Negro acts that way—for the good of Compton —he's going to be applauded for his civic mindedness, and he will be taken to task if he doesn't, but the white man can be as selfish as he likes and nobody will ever say to him, 'You only look out for yourself . . . Why don't you think about Compton?'

"You just have to understand that the white man still thinks that what's good for him is good for Compton.

"Part of the problem," Brice continues, "is Negro apathy. My people are so busy getting ahead, they just don't have the time, the money, or the know-how to get themselves deeply involved. So it always looks like the white man is more committed. Take school board elections. We had one last year in which a tax override was voted down. It was voted down because my people didn't vote. They needed the schools, but they didn't want to spend the money. We have Negroes on the school board, but it's still the most conservative element in town. And it's difficult to get qualified Negroes to run because they're so busy making it, and because many of them have the same attitudes as the whites towards spending public money.

"For example, we have one upper-middle-class neighborhood where mostly Negroes live. They have a lot of space. They raise horses. They like their privacies. Well, that's just fine, I suppose, but when you go to them about paying higher taxes, they have the same attitudes toward the lower-class Negro on welfare as the Colonel [the publisher of the local paper].

"I suppose it has to do with things like Watts. The whites are leaving, and the Negroes feel threatened too. Well, then, we've got to do something, don't we? *But what are we doing?* The truth is most of the whites don't hate us. I'll never believe that. They may not like us. Some may even prefer to live in trailer parks than to live among us, but some are stay-

ing on. It's surprising how many. There'll always be a few
whites in Compton. We just can't worry about those who
go away. We have to worry about ourselves. What are we
doing about the way this town is run? If Compton is becoming an all-black city, does it have to become Watts? *We need
a plan for now, not 1984, or this place will be just like Watts
by then.*"

SCATHERS:

Roy Scathers is a former noncommissioned officer of the U.S. Army from the state of Alabama, who retired
after twenty years of service and came to Compton with a
wife and child to work in one of the local banks. His salary
isn't large, but because of his pension he is able to live quite
well. Scathers is very popular in Compton among Negroes
and whites. He speaks with a broad Alabama drawl, and
sometimes cannot restrain himself from saying "Nigra" and
"Cawcasian," but most people seem to recognize in Roy's
case that the force of habit isn't necessarily a sign of malice.
When whites started leaving Compton in large numbers, he
was one of those who tried to reassure Negro action groups
that he would like to stay on. He did this, he explains, "because we're no longer in Alabama. I came to get away from
that kind of thing. It wasn't like that in the Army, and I don't
want it to happen here.

"But," Scathers continues, "it's happening just the same.
Don't you know why? It's because I'm white and Southern
and I've got my limitations and so do my Nigra neighbors.
It's just as if certain things have been built into you. You

better believe it. I don't hate anybody, but I worry a lot about my kids. I want them to stay white. Why? Because my family was poor white, and that's about all we ever had . . .

"You better believe it. The Nigra and Cawcasian are never going to lie down in the same bed together here in Compton, or any place else for that matter, but we could work together if we gave it half a chance. I mean, color can't be everything. I have as much in common with some of my Nigra neighbors as I do with the business folks uptown . . . the car dealers, I mean. But how is it ever going to come back? I mean Compton . . . What's going to happen to it? When Watts started burning, my wife and I were in Oakland visiting her stepsister. Folks asked us aren't you afraid for your house, and I said: 'My neighbors will keep an eye on it because they don't want anything to happen to their own property,' but I must say I felt pretty queasy—more so because those folks just gave me the big horselaugh . . .

"So you see what I mean. Nigras and whites like us have a basic distrust of each other, and there isn't too much individuals on their own can do about it. I'm willing to stick it out here just so long as some other whites do, and I'm even willing to try and do my bit to get others to do the same, but I feel awful lonesome sometimes. My Nigra friends say, 'When it comes right down to it, you're just like everybody else, Roy.' And the whites say, 'You've got a pension. You've got security. It's different with you.' You better believe it. I'm not typical. I'm getting less and less so, and everybody knows that."

179

SNART:

Carl Snart is a member of the Compton power elite. He owns one of the largest auto showrooms in the area, and that qualifies him for membership in a few of the various service clubs. His wife is also a sister of a former high town official.

Carl's parents came to Compton from Oklahoma during the depression. His father hired himself out at first to one of the Nisei farmers. Then he worked on the WPA. Carl joined the Army when the Japanese attacked Pearl Harbor and, after the war, studied business administration under the G.I. Bill at U.S.C. When an offer came from Cal Ozark to go to work in his auto showroom, Carl quit school and gladly accepted because the commissions were important to him; he saved his money and gradually bought into the business until, at Ozark's death, he was a half-owner. Then Carl bought out Ozark's widow and expanded his trade, keeping the name: Ozark and Snart.

Because of his ambition, Carl Snart was late in getting married. He was just too busy "improving himself," as he put it. But he now has three children, all of whom are attending a Catholic parochial school. This, despite the fact that Carl is a Baptist. "I just think it's better that way," he explains. "It isn't even a question of prejudice. I just don't think I have to cheat my kids to prove a point. A lot of merchants in town have moved out, and only come here to mind their trade or for Rotary, but I feel it wouldn't be right in my business to do any such thing. I mean, so much of it is public relations— Little League and all that sort of thing—and I've even got

Negro salesmen. That doesn't mean I have to expose my children to them. My kids deserve the best. I've worked hard. I can afford to do what I'm doing, and I'm going to do it whether my neighbors like it or not. When people say to me, 'Carl, I don't think that's such a good thing to do from a public relations point of view,' I tell them to mind their own business. Some people have a lot of nerve. And some people, I think, are just a bunch of Communists, whatever they may call themselves. I'll be specific, if you like. When I came to Compton, there were plenty of poor people here, but nobody bellyached the way these people do. We found work. We did things about it. Now we've got the Welfare and we've got the War Against Poverty, and people never stop bellyaching. Well, how would you like to live in a town that people say is a poverty area? It wasn't that way when I first came here. In those days Compton was a respectable town. Now it's a trouble spot, a poverty area. If I were smart, I'd move my family out of here, but I like my house. I like my neighbors. I don't mind paying for my kids' schooling. I just wish my business didn't demand that I live here. But that's the way it is. You want to make money off people, you got to live with them. It's always like that in a small town."

THE MINISTRY:

For many Comptonites, religion still has a great influence. Compton's citizenry is largely nonconformist Protestant, except for the Catholic* Mexican-American

* It was from one of Compton's large Catholic churches that Father William DuBay directed his attack on Los Angeles' aging Cardinal McIntire and asked that the Pope relieve him because of his racism. DuBay was later relieved of his priestly duties.

community, but there are so many sects and denominations encompassed by that all-encompassing term that the community is even less homogeneous (more nonconformist) than it might, at first, appear.

The oldest and most respectable church in Compton is the integrated First Methodist, near the Civic Center. In the Willowbrook area, there is a large active Negro congregation of Episcopalians. And throughout the streets of black and white Compton are fundamentalist Baptist missions, evangelical orders, pentecostal brethren, public ministers, faith healers, and the like.

"Blind—See/ Deaf—Hear/ Lame—Walk," a sign on a decrepit white clapboard structure reads as one goes out through the last remaining bastion of white exclusivism before the freeway bridge-crossing which leads into Paramount. In general, white religion is of the same unsophisticated variety as that which is preached within the Negro fundamentalist churches, but the two are strictly segregated from one another, as much so, in fact, as in the South. A white preacher explained why: "People came here to get away from that trouble back home. They came here so their children wouldn't have to live with Nigras. I think they have a right to decide those things for themselves. This country, after all, believes in freedom of religion."

But a black minister has a somewhat different view of the matter: "I respect a man who can damn a whole race in a single sentence, and that's what my fellow pastor of God has just done. Am I supposed to like it? You bet I don't. I've been in Compton ten years, and I don't think I've ever even talked to that man, and we're supposed to believe in the same truths about God. I remember, one morning, I was handing out church bulletins when I passed that preacher. He was just standing there outside his office. It was still quite early in the morning, and I expect he just didn't want to see me. Or me to see him. But I could tell he was curious. So I put a paper under his door and walked on. When I got around the corner, I looked back. I could see he was kind of curious. He sort of looked the other way, and then he grabbed for that paper with his hand . . . just like that . . . so it would look like I didn't see him. That's the way things are around here. We're supposed to be brothers, but we're so busy lying to each other.

"Well, I don't mind any of that, if only they would take care of their children, teach them a little decency and respect, teach them a little brotherhood. But all they teach them how to do is how to hate. You hear an awful lot about Negro kids getting into trouble, but I'm telling you the white kids are worse. They have no motivation to learn. They hate their parents. They're just plain no-good. Sometimes I'm sorry I have to have my kids integrating with them, because they learn a lot of bad things that way."

RUTH MANNIX:

Ruth Mannix has a face like <u>Queen</u> Nefertiti, and she dresses with queenly elegance, piling her straight black hair high above her sculptured forehead, her skin lustrously black, her clothes tailored and elegant. In her spacious back yard, three young children were at play with the maid. Dr. Mannix, an internist, would not be home from Los Angeles until late. She invited me to sit in one of her upholstered armchairs and offered tea or coffee, but, when I said that I would prefer nothing at the moment, she immediately reverted to what we had been talking about: black nationalism.

"You say integration," she declared, "well, just tell me this: with who am I going to integrate? With my neighbor next door? My husband and I go to see *Fiddler on the Roof* and are members of the Los Angeles Civic Museum, and she spends her wedding anniversary at the Palladium dancing to Lawrence Welk. No thank you."

Mrs. Mannix, who was not much over thirty, smiled prettily: "That's why I think my people have got to have their own culture . . . their own pride."

I asked, "Just what do you think you have in common with the mother on Welfare, over there in Willowbrook?" Then I glanced about the well-appointed room.

"We're both black," she was saying. "We're both black."

"Yes," I said. "But your children will go to college, and hers won't even finish high school."

"That's why we have to help ourselves," Mrs. Mannix smiled.

I was used to that smile by now. It was ultimately a deceit. Mrs. Mannix may have been a mover and shaker in all the local civic improvement associations, but like many ambitious middle-class women, she wasn't planning to tell me much about how she felt, or thought, what motivated her, or why she lived the way she lived. I didn't really blame her, except that she had begun all this talk about race. Why did it always have to end up in a flak of slogans? I had come to her to find out about life in Compton, but whenever I talked about Compton, I got a feedback about race. The white man felt he had a black noose around him, and the black man felt he had a white noose around him, and some black men in Compton also felt the added strangulation of the Watts noose. You couldn't duck it anywhere you went, not even in the courts.

The day before, I had gone with one of the town's leading attorneys, a white liberal, to Municipal Court, because he wanted to show me those who were being arraigned. *"And you say we don't have a color problem,"* he sneered, pointing at the predominantly black mass of youths in the dock. My white liberal attorney friend seemed to regard the ragged white offenders in their motorcycle jackets as mere abnormalities; it was the Negro who obsessed him. They seemed to obsess everybody in white Compton. I wanted to tell my lawyer friend about Noni and her family. I also wanted to tell Mrs. Mannix, but was afraid she would take offense. So I sat back and let her spout Malcolm X at me.

Mrs. Mannix was saying, "We're in Compton, we're black, and we're proud to be black. We don't want to mix with rednecks. We want to be black. We're not interested in integration twenty years from now. We want freedom and equality for the blacks of all America."

I asked, "How do you propose to get it?"

"The same way your ancestors did."

Although the chances were that her grandparents had

been more middle-class than mine, if I had raised such an issue she would have only explained that it was color that kept hers back. Kept them back from what? Where else did she want to go from here? But why not let her go wherever she pleased? After all, I had not come to inquire about her personal ruthlessness. Did Mrs. Mannix want power, or black power? Was she acting in her interests, or in those of the "black masses"? Again, I thought of how she had reacted when I asked what she had in common with the Watts mother on Welfare. Her reaction had been about as public-spirited as one might expect under the circumstances, considering the fact that my question was impertinent. Why did Mrs. David Mannix, prominent middle-class Negro activist, have to be even more impeccable in her motivations than white folks generally are? Once again, it had to do with that anomaly, black power. If only Mrs. Mannix were a tired old hack. But she was preaching something new, urgent, a vivid social doctrine. Did she really believe her own words?

JACK WASHBURN:

Jack Washburn is a guidance worker in downtown Compton. He has no formal training in social work, but is highly respected by teen-agers as a former local basketball star and a "regular guy." Washburn works with both whites and Negroes. Most of his clients are the sons of blue-collar workers and are lower middle-class school dropouts. He tries to put them in touch with various Federal job training programs, or convince them to go back to school, but, thus far, he admits he has had very little luck.

"You wouldn't believe it," Washburn explains, "my clients just aren't very anxious to do much of anything. They seem to distrust every training program. They don't seem to want to learn the things we want to teach them. One of my kids, for example, he can't hardly read or write, but when I got him this trainee job at a local nursing home, he was there for a month and they had to fire him, finally, even though they didn't want to, because he just never got up early enough in the morning. 'Talk to him,' they said. 'Try to tell him he should get up.' It didn't do any good. I had this kid down here and I said, 'You can't even read and write. What do you think is going to happen to you?' Well, this kid couldn't have cared less. He said, 'I'd like to have a job just like you have. I'd like to wear a suit and sit behind a desk and talk to people all day on the telephone. That looks like a nice job.'

"Try and make that kid understand that I had to do a lot of things like going to college. He couldn't care less. He didn't want to train, and he didn't want the schooling. He just wanted the money and the status."

"But don't get me wrong," Washburn said. "I'm not saying all my kids are like that. I'm just saying a surprising number are. Many more whites than Negroes, too. Negroes seem to have more motivation. But not all. It's just terrible to watch most of them. They go into a training program, and it's impossible for them to find any satisfaction out of the money they are given because they see everybody else spending so much more. Then they drop out and move somewhere else to collect the Welfare. Or they get delivery-boy jobs and go off on benders. It's just getting harder and harder for many of these kids to imagine that they will some day be living according to their version of the good life on what they think they can be expected to earn, so they find some pretty little girl who is working and they get married, and for a while all is beautiful with cars, new furniture, high-fi rigs, and then she gets pregnant and the honeymoon is over.

"I don't know what can be done about any of this, but I think we ought to recognize it for what it is. The kids I know just seem to believe that the world owes them a living. And they're not so very far from wrong, when you see the way some people are living. I drive a four-year-old car. Do you think I set a very good example for those kids?"

CONOVER:

Ben Conover is a Midwesterner who has taught in the Compton school system for nearly ten years. At present he teaches in Compton Union High School, which is more than 90 per cent Negro. He finds teaching Negro students challenging, and he has good things to say about their motivations and curiosities; he is also in close touch with many students from the white community. Ben is one of those teachers who is fond of rhapsodizing about his students as representing "the future," but, when pressed, he is often more skeptical than he seemed at first. "Education means a lot these days, and everybody knows it," Ben says. "You talk to my students, and they know it. How can they help it? We've literally been beating it into their heads ever since Sputnik.

"And for the Negro," Ben continued, "it's even more important, and they are aware of that too. My Negro students know from their parents what education can mean for them, and they are desperate to be achievers. No. You can't fault the parents. They've motivated these kids only too well. And you can't fault the kids either, because they come here anxious to acquire the know-how to become a part of our new technological society, and then we fall down on them, and some fail, and it's probably not their fault.

"It's a terrible tragedy. It's a tragedy that those with the talents don't succeed, and it's even more of a tragedy that success has become so important. I really don't know how to say this because it may sound prejudiced, when I mean it for the white kids as well. What I mean is, maybe it was better when not everybody had to engage in this ruthless competition. I just feel some are bound to be disappointed, even if they manage to succeed a little. I just think it's in the cards. For myself, I never worry that much about the bright ones who are discouraged a bit on the way to becoming a scientist or a writer, because I figure that if they really want to, they will, but I worry about the ones who are going to be somewhere in between the big successes and the failures. For the first time in human history, they've been sold the bill of goods that education can really change their lives in meaningful ways. Well, maybe it can, but why do people have to change that much? Why is it so necessary? I see my talented kids, and I know they can be pretty un-

189

feeling sometimes. Is that what we can expect in the future?

"Also, I ask myself, if education can do all the things they say it can do, what's going to become of Compton? Quite frankly, what's going to become of me? I mean people like me . . . I'm educated, sure, but only in a relative sense. It's a hard thing to accept that some of your kids are going to pass way beyond you. As grateful as you may be, it's still a damned hard thing. I guess some others have told you that there are many kids here who won't get anywhere. They have no drives—no ambitions. They've just about zonked out completely, one way or the other. Well, I don't sympathize with them, but I can understand what it must be like. If all we're doing is intensifying the rat race, why bother?

"But the majority of our kids here feel differently, and I can't say I blame them. It's the first opportunity their families have ever had, and they're anxious to take advantage of it. The ones who zonk out, who won't compete, who hang around the coffee houses in Venice, or the bars in Santa Monica, the Hell's Angels, acid heads, beats, you know, that sort of kid—it's hard to say much in their favor, but it's not so hard to see their big hang-up. Far too many of those kids have never known anything but sweetness and light. No wars! No depression! They've even had taken from them any objective state of reality by which they could measure their own achievements, and so they've zonked out.

"The poor boy sees the odds against him and tries to even them through his own efforts, but when the game has been rigged in advance for the middle-class kid it's sometimes a lot harder for him to know what his goal is. I see that all the time. Really talented kids of all sorts just aren't content with any of the achievements which could easily be theirs. It's got to be pure ecstasy or nothing. They're perfect little monads bumping up against one another. They've zonked out. They've had the good life, and it didn't seem to be that nice. Now they're out to search for it in their own fashion, but they've got no structure outside themselves by which to measure what they hope to achieve, and they give up trying.

"A lot of people worry about the Negroes, and I do too because they've got achievement coming to them, but I also worry about these white kids. They're too smart not to cause trouble, and too much a part of America to be left so far out of it. Whatever they are, we and their parents made them that way. They live in a world without hardships, and so they induce hardships and feel compassionate about the hardships of others, Negroes in particular, and they remain, in the end, perfect little solipsists, who are cynical about everything.

"Somebody else always seems to have the power. Somebody always seems to be ruling over their destinies, even when they go their own ways, and what I worry about is how tolerant the new achievers will be of such behavior when they gain the power which they have earned. I mean, won't there be a terrible showdown some time? I used to worry about this a whole lot about the time of Kennedy's assassination, because I thought Lee Oswald was a combina-

191

tion of both these types, but now I see the liberals say he didn't have anything to do with it. Well, some people are a whole lot smarter than I am, but I think I know certain things. And one thing I know is that a lot of Lee Oswalds have passed through my classes. It's a bitter thing to say, but I'm afraid it's true."

TWO STUDENTS:

Barney is white Protestant, good-looking, and athletic; Pedro (who insists his friends call him Pete) is Mexican, copper-colored, hawk-featured, and strongly built. They are both students at Compton Junior College, and they grew up together. Barney hopes some day to go on to one of the four-year state colleges and, eventually, study law or government. Pedro's ambitions are somewhat more limited: he's hoping to get a good enough background in business administration at Compton JC so that one of the large LA corporations will want to take him into their training program and groom him for a managerial position. At the moment, however, neither of them is doing very well in school, and it's not a matter of lack of intelligence. They each say they just don't have the interest. "It's this Vietnam thing," Barney says. "I feel like I'm only here so I can stay out of being there. It gets to you after a while. You don't like to spend your whole life dodging things . . . and yet I know I wouldn't be accomplishing anything by getting myself killed over there."

Asked whether he understood what the war was about, Barney, at first, said, "It doesn't matter very much what I think." Then he added: "I think it's stupid . . . the whole thing . . . and I think a lot of my friends do, too. Only you won't catch us saying any of those things. Who are we going to say them to? Besides, too many of our friends are over there already. In a place like this, you can't go around knocking things like that."

That's one of the reasons why Barney thinks he would like to leave Compton as soon as possible, but Pedro, more of an outsider to begin with, is more openly critical of the war and less anxious to make his home elsewhere. "It's very simple," Pedro says. "There is nobody around here who can work up any enthusiasm for a war in which the poor people are killing the poor for nobody's sake, but that doesn't mean nobody's going to do anything about it. People here know Orientals . . . and a lot of them, a lot of Mexicans I mean, grew up with them, and they don't find them so sneaky and devious as all that. That's why they don't work up that much anger about the Chinese. But when you find out that your neighbor's boy just got wounded or killed, what are you going to say? Are you going to tell him it wasn't worth it? Are you going to say the Americans are committing war crimes? That's why people around here don't have any use for the beatniks [anti-Vietnam war demonstrators]. They don't seem to feel sorry for anybody except themselves.

"Well, I mean," Pedro continues, "if there were the kind of people I respect in any of those demonstrations, maybe I would go out and do the same, but there just aren't those kind of people . . . and I agree with Barney, unless it's that

193

way, it makes you feel awfully guilty staying in school, because you know you're just wasting your time so you won't
get drafted. My mother says you're in school because it's a
great opportunity. And Barney's folks, they feel the same
way. But the fact is I can't look at it that way. I have to
tell myself—I guess we all do—that I'm staying in because
there's no percentage in being anyplace else. I'm lucky for
a change. It hasn't always been that way in my family."

"Pete's right," Barney says. "It never was so good for
most of us here. Most of the colored kids we knew, they're
in the service. And my brother was in Korea. I don't understand what people expect us to do. But I can't help feeling
guilty. It just doesn't seem right . . . I mean the whole
thing. Even our parents feel that way, but they'll never say
anything. Who would listen to them?"

I asked them how they regarded the Vietnamese people
themselves:

Pedro: People like that . . . if we didn't do it
to them, somebody else would. Don't get me wrong. I'm
not for bombing. I don't like the pictures I see. I just think
it's that kind of screwed-up country. I just wish the whole
thing would stop tomorrow. Don't ask me how.

Barney: Pete's right about those people. They
never had any real democracy like we learned about it in
school, and maybe when it's all over we can do something
to help them. But I'm not convinced that we will. All my
friends tell me it's a lot rougher over there than they say it
is on the TV. They come back and they say it's hell over
there, and that we're taking a terrible beating. Well, if that's

the case, I just wonder if it's worth it. I mean, what are we trying to prove? My parents say I'm just a dumb kid and I've got no business to say these things, but even they talk this way among themselves, and my brother who knows the score—because he was in Korea—he says it's all a lot of bunk that we're being fed. So that's why I figure why should I stick my neck out? For what? I'll stay here in school and listen to the teachers telling me how lucky I am not to be over there. The only thing I don't like is that they hold your grades against you. If you don't do too well, they can draft you anyway. That's a hell of a way to have to work . . . Did you ever try to get good grades when you knew that was happening?

Pedro: I can't help thinking that this whole thing doesn't make any sense. If the war ends, what will it all mean? If it doesn't end too quickly, what are we doing there in the first place? That's why I think even my people —Mexican people—sort of agree with the Colonel when he says to drop an atom bomb on them and get it over with. I mean, nobody likes to see anybody getting hurt. What do you think is happening right now?

Barney: I can't agree with that kind of talk. We wouldn't like it if it happened to us.

Pedro: It never could happen in a place like this.

Barney: I think they ought to try to end the whole thing. People won't like it, but they ought to do it anyway. How? Well, I think they ought to make those people listen to reason.

195

Pedro: How are you going to make a bunch of fanatics listen to reason?

Barney: I'm not so sure they are fanatics. I mean we say so, but how do we know? How can we be sure? I would just like to get it over with one way or the other. It just seems rotten to have to waste your life like this waiting for something to happen. It's just rotten . . . and I really resent it when people like my parents tell me I'm lucky. I can't take any chances. I can't make any plans. What's so lucky about that?

Pedro: I think it's all that Johnson's fault. He's just not the kind of man I would trust.

Barney: Don't kid yourself, Pete. It was Kennedy who got us in this mess . . .

Pedro: But Kennedy was a bigger man. Everybody says so. You know what I mean?

Barney: Maybe so . . . Actually, it was Eisenhower who got us in there. So, you see, it's like one big mess and there isn't anybody you can really trust. That's why a lot of our friends are so bitter. I mean, it looks like nobody ever thinks any more . . .

Pedro: I think they think too much. I think Johnson is a big schemer.

THE KOZYKS:

Rose and Arthur Kozyk are an interracial couple living in a housing development about two miles east of the Compton city limits. Their postal address is Compton, but the Kozyks think of themselves as living simply in a housing development. They are from the East, and they don't seem to mind the anonymity of tract living. The place is thoroughly integrated, which means that it is largely Negro. They have one little girl of six, and they are proud homeowners.

When they first ran off together, the Kozyks inhabited a walk-up flat in Chicago's Old Town. It was grimy and uncomfortable, and Rose says all their white liberal friends seemed uncomfortable with them. Now, like Denny Robbins, they seem to luxuriate in anonymity. Arthur works in a direct-mail advertising firm, and in his spare time he tries his hand at serious writing. Rose works as a substitute teacher when she can find somebody to look after her daughter. Rarely do the Kozyks find themselves going into Compton Center. They take car trips. They spend a lot of time at the beach. Occasionally, a niece of Rose's, who lives in Pacoima, can be cozened into driving down to baby-sit, and they will go out to dinner or to the movies in Los Angeles.

About the life around them, the Kozyks say they are as oblivious as they can be. "Our neighbors are very different from us," Rose says. "They're not bad people, but we don't have too much in common." Arthur adds: "All I know about Compton is that the police wear patches on the sleeve saying: HUB CITY. And all I know about my neighbors is that they're just about like everybody else. They work hard. They worry about their kids. Some of the men get

197

drunk or difficult sometimes. Some of the women are a little smug. It's not what I would call a community, and that's just as well. If it were, Rose and I might not be able to take too much of it . . ."

"Only time it was anything like that," Rose interrupted, "was during the riots. Don't kid yourselves. All of us here felt threatened. It was terrifying. The men all had guns. We slept on the floor, with the lights out and the doors locked. On the second night, it died down. Then it got worse again. People said they were coming this way. I told Art, 'Don't worry about my feelings. If you have to shoot to kill, you must shoot to kill. You must protect us.'

"I know a lot of Negro women who told their men the same thing because, you see, when something like this happens, are you going to stand out there and say I'm black to a bunch of crazy animals? I don't think it would have mattered one bit. Afterwards, Art and I thought of leaving the place, but it just didn't seem practical. We have the place at a very reasonable price, and we can be happy here if we mind our own business. We didn't come here out of choice. We didn't even know where we were going. We happened to see an ad for the house, and there was no down payment, so we moved in. I'm not sorry we did. I'll never be sorry for that. Maybe it's just a little harder on Art. After all, I never had much of anything, and this is surely a hell of a lot more than that. But Art had a family life. It wasn't so good, but it was a family life. I suppose this is a big step down for him, although I don't think he feels that way. The truth is," Rose added, "we have never talked about any of these things until now. We love each other, and we relate to each other, and that's an awful lot more than I can say for a lot of people."

"The truth is," Art contradicts, "she and I and the kid can take it here because we know the place doesn't have anything to do with us . . . and that's the truth."

CHAPTER IX

AFTERWARD

I t is about time that people stopped
moving to California. They have been doing it for years
now; consider its effect on the rest of America. Consider its
effect on Compton. It is about time that people stopped
dreaming about the place, stopped holding California out
for themselves as that one extra option when the life they
lead somewhere else becomes bleak. Then Californians will
be able to look around and see where they are living, and
what they propose to do about it. Perhaps then, too, California will finally have a chance to settle down and be something.

In an increasingly elitist country like America, there really
is no good reason why people should want to stay tied to
the familiar, to things such as class and neighborhood. Yet,
when we transcend them, we leave behind a detritus of bit-

terness and envy. There is also the fact that we betray the poor—and all those others who follow us and to whom we still claim some allegiance—into the hands of the bitter ones who linger on, those least able to do anything but hate them. Consider the protests of the students of Berkeley, most of whom intend to leave places like Compton far behind. Their case against the injustices of technopol America is strong (and they have demonstrated deep concerns about the Negro, the war in Vietnam, etc.), but it is the very elitism to which they aspire which has ensured the demise of Compton; and Compton's demise is a black, as well as a white, disaster.

For it is getting harder and harder for the black man to aspire even to Compton when he looks around him and sees the way the white man's children feel about it. But Negro poverty at present also guarantees that Compton will be about the most immediate option for black men, and for many years to come. And then they get there, and they also turn bitter, because their new neighbors are, in the main, the bitter whites who have been left behind. What this ensures, of course, is that there will always be someone on the bottom, a class who must be planned for by the others who assume all the power and the prerogatives, and that theirs will be the legacy of bitterness which those on the bottom have always had for aristocrats. Most important of all, such elitism and what it does to places like Compton is the best way I know of breeding a kind of home-grown fascism, even if the ruling ideology appears to be liberal.

201

There is a wall going up already around California. It is an elitist wall, a self-ghettoization, a wall of expertise and ease such as one finds around the Center for the Study of Democratic Institutions in Santa Barbara. These rational men are trying to reconstruct Athenian society inside a political vacuum. They are men of intelligence, too, but because they simply refuse to acknowledge the brutish, the unreasonable, in short, power, they remain about as effective as chemists studying elm tree blight. While I was in Compton, for example, they were recommending an immediate end to economic need through the guaranteed annual income for all, while Los Angeles Mayor Samuel Yorty was quarreling with the local citizenry over whether they should pay to have their garbage collected.

In an odd way, I enjoyed being in Compton, but I am honest enough to admit that it was only because I also knew I would be getting away. My last day in town seemed to recapitulate my arrival there. Shortly before leaving, I went to purchase a subscription to the Colonel's newspaper. A thin woman with a big pouch of skin under her chin took the order, accepting my check without so much as a question, but, when I gave her my New York address, she glanced up, as if requiring some further explanations.

"It just happens," I lied, "that I'm interested in keeping up with Compton."

"I don't see why," she said, flatly.

I would have been content to leave it at that, except that her glance remained inquiring. At last, she asked, "You like it here?"

I tried to nod at her politely.

"I find that a little hard to believe," the woman said, handing me a receipt. Then she considered me again, as if to measure the extent of my deceit. "I don't know," she said, at last, "you seem like a decent young man."

I said, "I came here on business."

Smiling, she said, "I guess if you were here on business, that wouldn't be too bad."

Later, outside on the street, I ran into Melvin Tenson, looking even more indignant than usual: "You ought to get on over to the City Clerk's office."

I asked why.

"To ask about construction permits," Tenson exploded. He said that they had dropped once again during the previous month to a new low of under 350. "And they just keep dropping," Tenson said, shielding his eyes from the sun with one hand. "I've never seen anything like it. Pretty soon it won't even be worth practicing law here in town. First, they took away our own Superior Court and moved it to the Civic Center. Now they're going to leave us high and dry without any law business."

I was beginning to think that Tenson was just one of those chronic complainers that you sometimes meet in small towns, except that we were standing in front of a local realtor's office and I happened to glance into the dusty storefront just then as the only man in the office, a Negro, seated behind a big gray metal desk, yawned, stretched out his arms, got up, went over to the front window and drew the blinds a little so that the sun would not be streaming in. Back at his desk a moment later, he cradled his head in his folded arms and seemed to go off to sleep.

Tenson had followed my glance. He said, "Watts was once like this."

. . .

The only bookstore in Compton is a fairly recent addition to the town. Operated by Negroes, it's just a couple of blocks away from the border separating white and black Compton. It is not a prosperous looking store. It has not even had time to be musty. It is just a little bare. Yet, one can find some decent editions of the classics on its shelves, and paperbacks about civil rights, along with a rather large collection of non-books, game-books, joke-books, how-to-do-it books, and best-sellers.

Before leaving Compton, I went to that store to buy a farewell present for Noni. The saleslady showed no surprise at my choice, but was rather perplexed when I asked if she could wrap it as a gift. It seems there wasn't any gift paper, not even any plain brown wrapping paper. "Most people just don't seem to care," she said. Then, pointing to one shelf which consisted largely of sex manuals, she added: "We don't get a big call for gifts here."

. . .

Later, after handing Noni her gift and saying good-bye at some length, I drove out along Rosecrantz Boulevard a final

time, following the gaudy billboards in the direction of Del
Amo Hills Estates, a new development of rather expensive
tract homes to which many "better" Compton Negro families were said to be moving. The drive was longer than I
expected, and I presently found myself moving through a
great stretch of vacant land with only bulrushes and oil der-
ricks to break the monotony. The air was damp. I could
smell the sea. In the distance, I saw the raw wood frames of
the new development, entirely surrounded by further fields
of bulrushes. Their isolation was assured, for there was
literally nothing else in sight but more fields, scattered
pumps, an abandoned car, and the already completed portions of the tract which lay half hidden behind man-sized
walls of stucco and concrete block. The radio said, "Beautiful Southern California where every day is a rhapsody," but
I wasn't put off by that any longer. I thought of Noni.
Within a few days, her brother-in-law, his wife, and the
children would be arriving, and they would be staying with
her until they found accommodations. Before I'd left, Noni
told me, "I'm just sorry you missed Bill. You and he would
have gotten on well."

Then I repeated how pleased I was to know her.

"I'm sorry if there was a lot of ruckus here," Noni said.

I said, "After a while, I was pretty comfortable."

She smiled: "I'll tell you a story about being comfortable.
Blake used to be a barber, not by trade, although he's better
than most professionals. Anyway, one day this particular
friend of ours brought his little boy over to get a haircut.
Meanwhile, he decided to get comfortable while waiting on

Blake to get through cutting his boy's hair, so he took off his shoes and laid across our bed in the bedroom where Blake and his boy were. I didn't mind at all because this guy is very intelligent—well-educated, owns a beautiful home, and also happens to be very attractive and wouldn't dream of destroying or dirtying anything, plus he's been knowing me all my life and knew Blake too . . . a long, long time.

"This guy is 36 and, like I said, I didn't mind at all because I like intelligent people but not intelligent snobs and this guy is far from being a snob, and is such a decent guy, but I could tell that Blake didn't like it at all to have this guy lounging on our bed. He kept giving him the eye, unnoticed by the guy. I guess Blake didn't care how long he had been knowing him or who he was, *he just didn't want him on our bed.*"

Noni smiled. "But now," she added, "if he had been a woman, things would have worked out just fine.

"But," she added again, "you couldn't meet a better person than Blake.

"But," again she smiled, "I'm different. I like people to get comfortable with me. A woman or a man could lounge on our bed all they liked, because if I like them it's perfectly O.K. . . .

"Take care of yourself," Noni had said then. Hugging one of her children close to her, she had waved good-bye as I drove out onto the street.

But now, circling the walled-in Del Amo Hills Estates in all their flat ugly raw newness, I could still hear Noni's voice almost like a chastisement: *"Blake didn't care how long he had been knowing him or who he was, he just didn't want him on our bed."*

Then the station's mobile news unit broke in with a special interview with one of the leaders of the social workers' strike. A flat, slightly nasal voice was trying to parry questions: "We try to understand . . . we try to be very non-judgmental with all our clients . . ."

At last the news came on: "Republican gubernatorial candidate Ronald Reagan today defended himself against the charge of political amateurism by describing his long years of public service as president of the Screen Actors' Guild . . .

"In Sacramento, meanwhile, Governor Pat Brown was getting ready for a helicopter excursion through the San Joaquin Valley in search of votes . . .

"And a group of white college students in Grenada, Mississippi, has declared 'We support Black Power!'

"Those are the headlines. Now here are the top stories . . ."

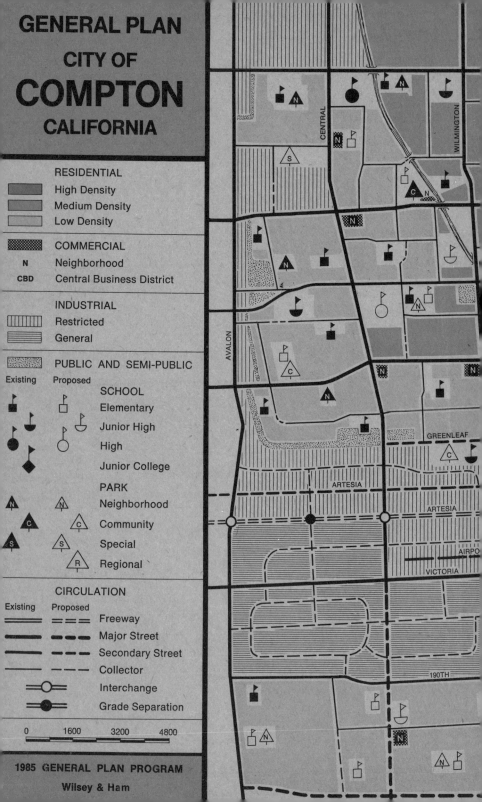